The Science of Intelligent Decision-Making:
How to Think More Clearly, Save Your Time, and Maximize Your Happiness.

Destroy Indecision!

By Peter Hollins
Author and Coach
PeteHollins.com

Table of Contents

The Science of Intelligent Decision-Making: How to Think More Clearly, Save Your Time, and Maximize Your Happiness. Destroy Indecision!.. 3

Table of Contents.. 5

Introduction 7

Chapter 1. What Drives You?...................................... 13

Chapter 2. Primed for Good Decisions 43

Chapter 3. The Six Hats Method and WRAP......... 61

Chapter 4. Making Calculations 87

Chapter 5. Mental Checklist.................................... 103

Chapter 6. Decision Traps 119

Chapter 7. Decision Traps Part Two 135

Chapter 8. How to Beat Analysis Paralysis and Indecision... 151

Chapter 9. Inevitable Emotions............................. 169

Conclusion 191

Summary Guide.. 193

Introduction

During my fourth and final year of college, I was guilty of making some fairly bad decisions.

Some of them are unfit to be public and involve cans of spray paint and silly string, but one of them was about the apartment I shared with my friends.

We had been looking for about two weeks for a new apartment because our current place was starting to show its age and our lease was almost up. We viewed listing after listing and attended a few open houses until I finally couldn't take it anymore. No one could make a decision about anything. It wasn't so much that we needed the place, but I was frustrated and my impatience took over my brain. I took it upon myself to speed up the process and push a decision.

When it was finally down to two apartments, I heavily pushed one of the apartments, and everyone was on board and took my recommendation so they could get back to their busy lives.

At first glance, this sounds like a story about decisiveness and taking charge, but it's really quite the opposite.

One of my roommates had a dog—a little chihuahua named Banana—that was our apartment's mascot. Every other apartment we looked at was completely fine with dogs, but the apartment I chose was most definitely not. I overlooked this crucial factor in my eagerness to be done with the process. We contemplated sneaking him in and out of the building for a year but decided it was not in our best interests.

What ended up happening was that I confessed to our future landlord, and we had to pay an extra $100 a month. When I say "we" I mean "I" because I footed the bill on account of it being solely my mistake.

The biggest sin I committed in this decision-making gaffe was assuming that I had all the information. I was lazy. I relied upon an assumption and didn't do the legwork to confirm or deny the assumption. I also struggled under the burden of making the decision for two other people (and a dog) and felt stress and anxiety from the pending deadline.

It was a perfect storm for me to miss an important detail that cost me over a $1000. Decision-making isn't necessarily an art form, but there are very specific ways that human beings can make incredibly suboptimal decisions without even knowing.

The consequences of my mistake with the apartment were relatively small, but what if I had been working on a huge deal with international corporations? There wouldn't be any recovering from that. You simply wouldn't be able to approach the deal without safeguards, processes, and double-checking. But we almost never do those things in our daily lives.

So how we can make better and more optimal decisions more frequently and avoid the internal and external traps that hold us back in life? Do we need to draw up a complex decision matrix for every fork in the road we come upon? Thankfully not.

We can do it by diving into the science and psychology of decisions. What has research shown and what does that mean for us? Why are the evolutionary drives that kept us alive harmful to use in this day and age? What are the roles of emotion and logic in decision-making, and should they be different?

Most importantly, why do I still order hamburgers even though I need to lose weight?

This book presents a thorough view of the decision-making landscape and teaches you how to make effective and intelligent decisions through a variety of methods, whether you have perfect information or not. What does beating indecision and becoming more confident in my decisions require? That's what lies ahead.

Chapter 1. What Drives You?

Decision-making is a term that means different things to different people.

I'm not just talking about how people might define it. I'm talking about the wide variance in driving forces behind people's decisions— the *why* of why people do what they do. What compels one person to do X can be the exact thing that compels their next-door neighbor to the opposite of X. You might rate X as your highest priority and determining factor, while your mother might rate X as an instant deal breaker that will bring shame to the family.

Decision-making affects us all differently because we are different people. We might be similar superficially—we all wear blue jeans and like showers. We want jobs that make an amount of money that will leave us comfortable, but we don't want to work long hours. We generally like our families and don't wish physical harm to most people. Those are all shallow factors that we are indeed similar in.

One of the first factors to consider in any decision is the motivation behind it. These differ drastically in each individual, whether they realize it or not. Specifically, most of what influences our decisions and everyday actions are subconscious needs and desires that you are probably unaware of.

These are the motivations and reasons that we instinctually act upon yet may not be able to articulate when pressed to clarify. These are what comprise the "gut feelings," "hunches," or flashes of insight that seemingly come from nowhere. It's because we all have different subconscious needs vying for dominance in our head that seek to influence our actions for greater happiness. You may be able to consciously articulate that you want to eat Chinese food tonight, but that's a one-off decision, whereas your subconscious needs create a unique pattern of behavior.

Unsurprisingly, subconscious desires and motivations have been studied heavily by psychologists over the years. For a brief glance, Sigmund Freud and Ivan Pavlov represent some of the most fascinating findings about our subconscious selves that we listen to far more than our conscious thoughts.

Pavlov is generally considered the discoverer of classical conditioning on account of his experiments with his dog. He paired feeding his dog with ringing a bell, and after a few weeks, his dog salivated at only hearing the bell. Of course, the dog was unaware of how he associated the food with the bell—we are similarly controlled and influenced by factors that we don't consciously realize.

Freud popularized the notion that we are ruled by childhood events, and there are three parts to our personalities. They are called the *id*, *ego*, and *superego*, which all have varying motivations that tear us in different directions. Our conscious thoughts are only a result of internal forces at war and who is winning at that particular moment.

If subconscious desires contribute to our decisions more than we previously realized, then it's clear we have to examine the existing models to categorize them. This allows us to understand what our potential range of needs and desires are, so you might be more aware of what you are influenced by and what you ultimately rely upon to make your decisions.

It's an attempt to make the subconscious more conscious; in essence, you are thinking about your thoughts so you can better understand yourself.

The three models of subconscious desires and needs are Maslow's hierarchy of needs, Tony Robbins's matrix of human desires, and the Max-Neef model of fundamental human needs.

Maslow's Hierarchy of Needs

Abraham Maslow's primary theory is that human beings are a product of a set of basic needs, the deprivation of which is the primary cause of most psychological problems. He encapsulated his findings into a hierarchy, which maps out basic human needs and desires and how they evolve and change throughout life. Your location in the hierarchy at any given time is what influences your subconscious needs and desires.

The hierarchy functions like a ladder. If you aren't able to satisfy your more basic foundational human needs and desires, it is borderline impossible to move forward to the next ladder rung without profound stress and dissatisfaction in life. The higher you are on the ladder, the more of your physical and security needs are taken care of, at which point you start yearning for psychological needs.

To illustrate, let's briefly look at how our needs change from infancy to adulthood. As infants, we don't feel any need for a career or psychological satisfaction. We simply need to rest, be fed, and have shelter over our heads. Feeding and survival are our only real needs and desires (and changing diapers as parents of newborns will tell you).

As we grow from infants into teenagers, simply staying alive and healthy doesn't bring satisfaction. We hunger for interpersonal relationships and social fulfillment. What drives us is to find a feeling of belonging and community. Then, as we mature into young adults, simply having a great group of friends is no longer enough to satisfy us. It feels empty, actually, without an overall sense of life purpose. We don't like to feel aimless and like every day is the same as the one before it.

If, as young adults, we are fortunate enough to be able to provide financial security and stability for ourselves and our families, then our desires and needs can turn outward rather than inward. It's the same reason that people such as Warren Buffett and Bill Gates start participating in philanthropy to make as big an impact as they can on the world. This is not a stage that everyone will reach in their lives, unfortunately.

As you can see, only when you can satisfactorily accomplish one stage can you move on to addressing the next, higher, and more psychologically fulfilling stage. You can't very well be giving all of your money to charity if you don't feel secure in your own basic needs. Simply put, the stages of Maslow's hierarchy of needs are why you feel unsettled and uncomfortable at work if you are at risk of eviction from your apartment. Your apartment represents your more fundamental need for survival and safety, while your work represents a relatively secondary need.

The stages of the hierarchy are as follows—remember that where you are in the hierarchy is what tends to influence your decisions more than you may realize.

Physiological Fulfillment. This is easily seen in the daily life of an infant. All that matters to them is that their basic needs for survival are met (i.e., food, water, and shelter). Without security in these aspects, it is difficult for anyone to focus on satisfaction in anything else. It would actually be harmful to them to seek other forms of satisfaction. This is the baseline level of fulfillment that must first be met. This is logical, because nothing else matters to you if you are homeless or starving.

Safety. You might call this stage security. If someone's belly is full, they have clothes on their back, and they have a roof over their heads, they need to find a way to ensure that those things continue. They need to have a secure source of income or resources to increase the certainty and longevity of their safety. The first two stages are designed to ensure overall survival. Unfortunately, many people never make it out of these first two stages due to unfortunate circumstances, and you can plainly see why they aren't concerned with fulfilling their potential.

Love and Belonging. Now that your survival is ensured, you'll find that it is relatively empty without sharing it with people that you care about. Humans are social creatures, and studies have shown that living in isolation will literally cause insanity and mental instability, no matter how well fed or secure you are. This stage includes relationships with your friends and family and socializing enough so you don't feel that you are failing in your social life.

Of course, this stage is a major sticking point for many people. They are unable to be fulfilled or focus on higher desires because they lack the relationships that create a healthy lifestyle. Isn't it easy to imagine someone who is stuck at a low level of happiness because they don't have any friends?

Once you reach this level, you start living outside of yourself. You start seeking something bigger and higher than yourself, in part because you don't need to account for yourself as much anymore.

Self-Esteem. You can have relationships, but are they healthy ones that make you feel confident and supported?

This stage is all about how your interactions with others impact your relationship with yourself. This is an interesting level of needs because it boils down to self-acceptance. You know you have a healthy level of self-esteem when you can accept yourself even if you are misunderstood, or outright disliked, by others.

For you to get to this stage and have a healthy level of self-esteem, you have to have accumulated certain achievements or earned the respect of others. There is strong interplay between how you get along with others and help others and how you feel about yourself.

Self-Actualization. The highest level of Maslow's hierarchy is self-actualization. This is when you are able to live for something beyond yourself and your needs. This is where people chase self-fulfillment and find their destinies, so to speak. When people finally have the foundations of a great life, suddenly that is no longer enough for personal satisfaction.

This is the stage people are at when they say they want to find their calling and purpose in life. They now have the luxury to ruminate on these issues, as opposed to worrying about where their next meal will come from. They can focus on a project, idea, or concept that is above their own petty, self-centered concerns. These are people who can set aside their own needs and work for or toward something that is beyond their mundane and self-serving concerns.

Sadly, many of us may never make it to this stage because we haven't fully satisfied the needs of the prior stages. It is a very privileged position to be in and shouldn't be taken for granted.

If you can accurately pinpoint where you fall in this hierarchy, it will let you know immediately what is going on in the background of your decisions. For example, if you are facing eviction, many of your actions will probably be oriented toward preventing that situation, and you won't care about your friendships for the time being. You must first feel safe and secure before wanting to socialize.

Maslow's hierarchy gives us a template for diagnosing ourselves and what occupies our mental bandwidth more than we might think. You may be stuck at stage one—physiological fulfillment. If so, you might feel like you just need to get everything together and focus on yourself for a while. You're searching for resources and security, and your decisions will (and should) reflect that.

Can you ascertain whether you are having issues with the following? (This is the hierarchy starting from the bottom.)

- Survival
- Security in accommodation and employment
- Personal and familial safety and health
- Relationships and friendships

- Romantic relationships and sexual intimacy
- Self-esteem and confidence
- Acceptance of self
- Self-actualization and fulfillment

If you are struggling with one stage, you know that nothing above or further than that stage matters to you. Whatever your concern is will color your perception, analysis, and decision-making on a subconscious level.

Maslow's hierarchy is just one framework of looking at your subconscious needs. The next framework is Tony Robbins's six fundamental human needs.

Tony Robbins's Six Fundamental Human Needs

This framework comes from famed motivational speaker, Tony Robbins. These six needs drive our lives in ways that we can articulate and others that we would never have thought. Again, understanding what your primary needs are will give clarity as to what's going on in your brain during tough or even daily decisions.

According to Tony Robbins, we generally value two out of the six needs the most at any given time. These two primary needs play a tremendous role in the kind of choices and decisions we make, as well as the habits we develop on a daily basis.

If you can understand these subconscious desires, you can make better decisions and short-circuit your negative impulses and emphasize your positive ones.

The Need for Certainty. The need for certainty is about the assurance that you can avoid pain and gain pleasure, which is best done through routine and stability.

The more certain and secure we feel in the predictability of our well-being, the more comfortable we feel engaging in other activities. This is why we crave predictability and assurance in our lives. These are very important because they ensure one extremely important goal: survival.

The more certain we are that there is no danger, the more we can relax to focus on other needs. Certainty forms the bedrock of our hierarchy of needs. Certainty ensures survival, and once this is taken care of, we can then look toward other needs.

However, the other side of the spectrum is when you feel certainty has been established. Think about it. Would you want to watch a basketball game if you already knew the score and everything that would happen in that game? Probably not. That would be boring and predictable.

Everyone requires different levels of certainty in their lives. For example, my own need for certainty is very low compared to others. I travel constantly and always have new hobbies. If things become too routine, I get bored very easily. I need to constantly challenge myself with the next need, which is in direct conflict with the need for certainty.

The Need for Uncertainty and Variety. The mirror opposite of the need for certainty is the need for the unknown and variety. This is the need for change and new stimuli.

We all need a change of scenery every now and then. The idea of novelty is attractive for a reason, and it's simply to experience something new and be surprised at an outcome rather than know it before you begin.

Do you want to watch the same type of movie over and over? Most people don't, but if you do, you might gather that you have a low need for uncertainty and variety. Too much uncertainty brings us fear, but not enough uncertainty will bring us a lack of fulfillment.

It's why most people enjoy traveling and eating new foods. We don't want to do the exact same thing over and over again. This is what makes life exciting, because we don't know what to expect. We have a need for the adrenaline that only novel stimulation can bring us. Routine is death (for some).

Variety brings pleasure even though it may result in a lesser chance of safety and survival.

The Need for Significance and Uniqueness. Deep down we all need to feel that we are important, unique, and special. We don't want to feel insignificant and that no one cares about us.

We want to be the special snowflakes that we like to imagine we are. We all want to stand out in a positive way and be known for something.

This is manifested in many different ways. Some will go out of their way to achieve in an academic sense, deriving their sense of worth in that realm. Everyone creates an identity of themselves based on their self-perception of how they're special.

If you've noticed someone that appears to be dressing solely for attention, they're taking pride in their unique appearance. They feel significant because they stand apart from everybody else.

No one would state their goal is to be indistinguishable from their neighbor, so this is a very natural inclination. However, taking things too far to the extreme can turn off most people. You can imagine this in the form of people who dress obnoxiously or who constantly feel the need to discuss how different they are.

Additionally, if you strive for too much significance and differentiation, you may relate to others less and less, which makes the next human need difficult.

The Need for Connection. We all have an instinctual need to bond and connect with others. We strive for interpersonal relationships because they make us feel validated, important, and social. We want to feel like we belong and are part of a tribe.

Some people are extremely family-oriented and travel in packs, where others are lone wolves that enjoy their own company. Some of us like to play team sports, while others like to run alone along the beach. There's a happy medium somewhere for everyone.

The basis for most of these connections is similarity and familiarity. You might call that convenience or opportunity, but the truth is that most relationships start there and evolve from that point.

It's easier to like somebody who is somewhat similar to you, because you can better relate to them. It feels more natural. This is why I mentioned earlier in our need for significance that we can't overdo things to such an extent that we destroy all similarity. We can be different, but not too different; otherwise, you're only going to connect with other outliers.

The need for significance versus connection is like trying to feed Goldilocks stew. If our need for connection is not being met, we feel alone and disjointed from people. However, if it's met entirely, we no longer feel different or unique, and we end up lacking a sense of significance.

The Need for Growth. Everybody is looking to expand and increase capacity and capabilities.

Everybody is looking to achieve their goals and move onto the next. Very few people are content simply watching television every day and starting the process over on the next. Most of us need a sense of progress and enjoy working toward something.

Everything on earth either grows or dies— that's not a false dichotomy. Human beings are no exception to this. We must feel we're constantly growing in our lives and moving forward.

The real litmus test occurs when you achieve a goal you set for yourself. Maybe it was a certain financial target, a certain lifestyle, or that new computer. Are you satisfied and no longer feel the need to keep reaching, or do you move the goal posts and start to plan how to exceed your original goal?

Those with a strong need for growth will be unhappy until they set a new goal because they're not growing anymore. To many of us, living life from day to day without an overarching goal and theme becomes an exercise in futility.

The Need for Contribution. Finally, we all have the need for a sense of contribution to society.

It might be a service to our community or giving money to a cause, but deep down, we all want to feel that we make an impact and won't pass from this earth without anyone caring. We want to make a mark on the world in our time and be memorable by contributing to society as a whole.

How many people will attend our funerals, and how much will they care?

This explains the popularity of volunteering and philanthropy. It's a universal need that exists in varying degrees in people. We want to give and contribute to a greater good above ourselves simply because it feels good and fulfills our sense of contribution to the world.

When you see a homeless person, do you feel compelled to give or do you ignore them? Do you want your work to affect thousands of people, or are you content just working for yourself?

This entirely different set of subconscious needs and desires, again, vary in each person, even if they appear to manifest the same. For example, your friend might be exercising fanatically because they have a need for certainty in their physical appearance and significance, but you might view exercise as fulfilling the need for personal growth. It is the same outward manifestation, but entirely different needs are satisfied.

On the other hand, you might have the same needs as someone else, but they are manifested in completely different ways. For example, you and your friend both have strong needs for uncertainty and variety. You fulfill it through traveling, but they fulfill it through changes of romantic partners.

Evaluate which of the six needs resonate with you and try to identify how attempting to satisfy these needs influences your decisions on a daily basis. Self-understanding is paramount to success, because otherwise, you're just winging it.

Max-Neef Fundamental Human Needs

The third model of subconscious desires and needs that influences our decision-making comes from Manfred Max-Neef, a researcher and economist.

His model might be the most thorough and detailed, as it accounts for nine human needs. It's not arranged as a hierarchy, even though there are similarities to Maslow's model, and it can be said to capture more of people's different personality traits. The needs are as follows.

Subsistence. The need for subsistence drives us to focus on our physical and mental health, as well as our sense of security and stability. You want to focus on everything that enables your lifestyle and keeps you from being homeless. This includes financial means for most people as well. Your decisions will skew toward feeding yourself, clothing yourself, working, and setting these things into place.

Protection. The need for protection makes us want to feel cared for and safe. You want to feel secure in your plans, actions, and choices you can make for yourself. This is in both a psychological and physical sense.

Affection. The need for affection will make you seek out friends and relationships so you can feel connection and intimacy. This makes you social and express emotions when you might otherwise isolate yourself. You want to be loved and respected, both physically and mentally.

Understanding. The need for understanding concerns how you view the outside world. You want to make sense of it, and you accomplish this by studying, investigating, learning, and thinking. That way, you can satisfy your curiosity and build your intuition. We all want to feel like the world is predictable in a comforting way.

Participation. The need for participation is to feel that you have a place in the world. You are part of a web of people, places, and things, and they all depend on you to some degree. This makes you want to accept responsibilities, work, volunteer, become involved, collaborate, and work with others. The more intertwined in some aspects, the better. This makes us join clubs and the like, and it imbues us with a sense of purpose and duty.

Leisure. The need for leisure is essentially the need to relax and have fun. This is a necessary interlude, because otherwise, our bodies and brains would run at full capacity with our other obligations. That leads to undue stress and anxiety. You want to let go of concrete worries and let your imagination and sense of creativity run free. You want to play games, goof around, and play like a child that has no responsibilities. This is a need for unwinding and taking a break from reality.

Creation. The need for creation makes us want to test the limits of our capabilities. What are we capable of, and how inventive can we be? Everyone has a need to express themselves, and creating is one of the easiest ways to do that. Creating art, music, or whatever else allows you to use your talents to their fullest. This is a need for individualism and uniqueness.

Identity. The need for identity is about feeling that you belong and understanding everything that you belong to. This includes groups, subgroups, religions, workplaces, occupations, or hobbies. When you have a sense of belonging, you are no longer just yourself, and you can gain confidence and self-esteem from approval from others. It also allows you to determine your values and worldview. This is about being able to say what kind of person you are and being a distinct person in your own right.

Freedom. The need for freedom is about your personal ability to be free. This relates to how autonomous your decisions are and how much free will you can exercise. Are you allowed to pursue your passions, or are you restricted to a limited amount of choices? For that matter, are you restricted by other people, society, or your occupation?

You want to be able to explore open-mindedness and not simply listen to someone else's opinions. You want to be able to dissent, doubt, and disagree without consequence. This makes you feel intuitive and smart because you are using your own assessment.

Again, the significance of these three models is to increase the vocabulary and insight with which you can articulate what you want. If you know what you are driven by subconsciously, you will know major decision factors that you might not have seen otherwise. All told, you now have twenty filters through which your decisions can be made. If you are able to identify at least a couple in yourself, imagine the added insight you will have.

Takeaways:

- Often, decisions can be consciously articulated. If you want Chinese food for dinner, that's easy to justify. But for both quicker and bigger decisions, you are likely more influenced by your subconscious than you realize. The importance of knowing potential subconscious influencing factors is thus extremely high to deciphering your actions.
- There are three models of subconscious needs and desires, the first of which is Maslow's hierarchy of needs. He articulates the following needs: physiological fulfillment, safety, love and

belonging, self-esteem, and self-actualization. Identifying your location in the hierarchy is identifying your subconscious needs.

- The next model is Tony Robbins's six needs: love and connection, certainty, uncertainty and variety, significance, contribution, and growth. Unlike Maslow's hierarchy, these needs function like traits and are present in different quantities in people. Pinpoint your particular needs and understand your decision process better.

- The final model is the Max-Neef fundamental needs: subsistence, protection, affection, understanding, participation, leisure, creation, identity, and freedom. This functions similar to Tony Robbins's needs in that these needs are present in everyone but in different quantities.

Chapter 2. Primed for Good Decisions

The key to truly making good decisions is to understand how your brain processes decisions.

In the prior chapter, we covered the subconscious motivations that underlie your decision-making. These are factors that operate without your knowledge and are much more powerful than your conscious motivators.

As the name of the chapter denotes, here we are going to cover a few factors that set the grounds for better and more effective decision-making.

In 2014, Swiss researchers discovered the area of the brain involved during decision-making. It's mostly the prefrontal cortex, which includes functions such as planning, deciding, calculating, analyzing, problem-solving, and decision-making. These are generally known as executive functions. The prefrontal cortex is activated during all decision-related thinking, and yet, it is not infinite or unlimited.

Like our bodies, our brains have limits and cannot carry on forever. If we run a marathon, we grow tired and fatigued from over-use. Our muscles cramp, especially the muscles that are used over and over, such as the quadriceps and calf muscles. It's the exact same in the context of making decisions.

Ego Depletion

Our brains have a limited number of decisions we can meaningfully analyze and make, and the more decisions we look at, the more fatigued we get. The prefrontal cortex is like our calf muscle that grows tired and eventually stops working in the correct way.

At that point, you're likely to make a decision out of impatience or become frozen in your tracks.

This is a phenomenon more generally known as *ego depletion*.

Ego depletion is the idea that our mental resources for specific activities are limited. When the resources drain or are decreased, those specific mental activities perform poorly. It was first discovered in relation to self-control, where experiments (Baumeister et al., 1998) showed that subjects who resisted chocolate performed worse and gave up earlier on a puzzle task. In other words, ego depletion was in full effect, and the amount of self-control they exhibited in resisting the chocolate directly weakened their ability to persist with the puzzle task. Decision quality decreased quickly as ego depletion started to take place.

Once you get over the initial surprise that something as small as self-control can actively deplete your mental resources, you begin to find that it makes all too much sense. The brain requires energy to act and think. In fact, the brain requires up to 20% of our daily energy consumption, despite being only 2% of the mass of our bodies. It works hard, and the act of self-control is not something that's easy.

The thought process involved in the debate over indulging in chocolate or not can be quite lengthy, and as the experiment showed, it can eliminate your capacity for self-control and discipline in the future. It's easy to resist chocolate once or twice, but when you encounter the temptation repeatedly throughout the day, your self-control will likely erode, and it will become nearly impossible to say no—because your brain will run out of juice to do so.

Further support for the theory of ego depletion came in the form of feeding versus starving the brain, and then seeing what happened while using self-control.

Experiments showed that using self-control depleted the brain of glucose, it's primary energy source, and that ingesting sources of nutrition and glucose could reverse the ego depletion and energize people's sense of discipline and self-control. Self-control uses a significant amount of your brain's power reserves, and purely exercising self-control can make you function noticeably lower overall.

How does this relate to making decisions? Besides the fact that any important decision will probably involve a lot of self-control, ego depletion has its own special label in this context: *decision fatigue*.

Decision fatigue is when you make too many decisions and use up all of the mental bandwidth in your prefrontal cortex, leaving any subsequent decisions short-sighted or improperly analyzed. Your ability to make decisions is limited, so you must conserve it and know what trivial decisions to avoid or minimize.

Let's take the simple example of sitting down in a restaurant and opening up the menu. Unfortunately, the menu is about 12 pages, front and back. It unfolds like a map and has enough space to document the rise and fall of the Roman Empire.

This is going to be annoying no matter what, but let's imagine how you might fare in two scenarios.

In scenario one, it is Sunday morning and you are waking up fully rested; in scenario two, it is Tuesday night after a 12-hour day at a work conference. In the first situation, you might be willing to thumb through the menu for a few minutes to optimize your decision. In the second situation, you would probably give up and select the cheapest hamburger because you can't be bothered at that point in the day.

No matter how rational or thoughtful you might be, it's impossible to make decisions without decreased efficacy. If you make 20 decisions in the morning, you'll probably splurge on an entire pie for lunch, buy a new bathrobe on the way back to the office, and then become angry and irritable when someone asks you what kind of format you prefer your reports in.

You may not be aware that you're tired, and you might be physically fit and alert, but the lack of mental resources will usually push you onto one of two paths.

The first path is acting impulsively and missing or altogether skipping analysis and important factors. This may not matter if you're only trying to decide what to have for lunch. A hamburger or a taco won't have any long-term implications. However, there are plenty of scenarios in which the failure to consider every single factor can be either financially, physically, or mentally harmful.

The second path that stems from decision fatigue is to do nothing at all and postpone a decision for another day. This might make you feel better, but it usually causes more problems in the long run, especially if these are any time-sensitive considerations. It might feel like a relief to push things off, but it's not a reality in a life filled with duties and obligations.

It's clear in both cases that decision fatigue is a suboptimal choice and leads to even worse outcomes.

Something as small as having to think hard in the morning about what you're going to wear or thinking about what you are going to order at your local coffee shop—it's things as small and trivial as these that can seriously short-circuit and deplete our brains for the rest of the day. If it leads you to think, "Oh forget it, let's just pick one and get it over with," that's the effects of decision fatigue. They are small acts, but they have greater consequences than you'd think.

Combat Decision Fatigue

Decision fatigue can be easily drained, so the question is how to safeguard this reservoir of brain power to use when you need it. How can you keep yourself primed for big decisions as often as possible?

First, time your decisions wisely. You can do this in two ways: first, make your big decisions early in the day or week, and second, always make them after a break. If you make decisions early and well timed, you are doing what matters first before daily life robs you of energy. The purpose here is to make sure your brain fed is well fed and rested and generally functioning at a high level so you can properly analyze decision factors.

You can't do this if you are constantly harassed by trivial decisions beforehand or your brain is starved for glucose. Sleep on it, or eat on it. Don't rely on your self-control or willpower as the first line of defense. Instead of putting yourself in situations where you have to use them, conserve them by developing preemptive habits to reduce mental fatigue.

Second, you should try to get a sense of what is trivial in your day so you can either ignore it, consciously make a quick decision about it, delegate it, or automate it.

How do you know if it's trivial? If it's truly trivial, it won't matter if you ignore it, or the choices you make will have no ill effect that lasts longer than a few minutes. This is a tough step for most of us because we are trained to give our full and undivided attention to something, lest we perform it poorly. In a way, this point advocates simply seeing what you can get away with paying little attention to—for your decision fatigue's sake.

Trivial decisions should only be allocated a trivial amount of decision bandwidth, so just try to keep things proportional. If something doesn't impact your life, are you losing anything by not taking action, picking a "good enough" option, or delegating the power of the decision to someone else? Doubtful. Get it off your plate as soon as possible.

The overall aim of this point is to make fewer choices a day. Instead of even dealing with some decisions, you could also choose to automate them—in other words, pick only one option and stick with it for consistency and easy. In a sense, you are making rules for yourself to ignore your choices and stick with, for instance, one lunch, one outfit, one music playlist, and one method of doing things. This is the purported reason famous Apple founder Steve Jobs had a standard uniform of sneakers, a black turtleneck, and comfortable jeans. It was so he could avoid making decisions and save his brainpower for when he actually needed it. On a daily basis, this can truly accumulate.

When you can make parts of your life more predictable, you can focus on the fewer parts that are unpredictable.

Third, if you've got big, multipronged decisions to think about on Tuesday, act like an athlete. This takes the first step to the extreme. That means to prepare and rest for Tuesday and lay off the heavy activity on Sunday and Monday. Your mental resources always recharge, but they are easily depleted.

Get into battle mode and treat your brain like a muscle that you need for peak performance.

Fourth, when you're in the decision-making process, attempt to allot yourself more time than you think is necessary. The reason for this is twofold. First, you will always take longer than you think, and second, feeling rushed is bad for decision-making because it creates stress and anxiety. The latter point is far more important because it uncovers the role of anxiety and stress in decision-making efficacy.

They are *terrible* for it. Most recently, a 2016 study published in the *Journal of Neuroscience* found that anxiety disrupts prefrontal cortex neuronal functioning. Remember what this area is mainly involved in? That's right—decision-making and analysis of costs and benefits. Decisions made under stress are incredibly impulsive and ineffective, notwithstanding the fact that stress is simply one of life's greatest distractions.

Let's take the following scenarios. In Scenario A, you are in a foxhole during World War II and you are being shot at. Explosions are all around you, and the person to your left suddenly collapses to the ground. The rain is starting to pour, and your weapon stops working. Your foxhole starts flooding, and you can hear a tank roll closer and closer.

In Scenario B, you have just woken up by the natural sunlight, and on a table in the room is left a splendid breakfast. It has croissants, jams, jellies, juices, and a stack of eight pancakes. The window is open and you feel a gentle breeze that smells like fresh flowers and dew on the trees.

Which of those scenarios do you think you would be able to make a better decision in? Probably the one with less stress, fewer distractions, and more mental resources available.

There's also a plethora of evidence, most recently confirmed in 2014 in a study at Columbia University Medical Center, to suggest that impulsive and knee-jerk reactions usually turn out to be very bad or wrong. In the study, it was found that a delay of even half a second to one second more before making a decision exponentially improved the outcomes.

Taken together, it's very clear that stress, anxiety, and any type of pressure to make a decision are detrimental to making clear-minded, effective decisions.

Lower Transaction Costs

The final method of battling decision fatigue is to lower *transaction costs*. Transaction costs, or friction costs, is an economic term for the cost you must expend to be in the market. Whenever you do something, you have some sort of cost associated with it. The cost may be monetary, such as an investment to start a business. For us, it's tied to the *ego depletion* cost in our brain's continued functioning. These are simply the costs, or obstacles, you have to swallow to participate in making a decision.

When you make a decision, good or bad, you incur a cost. The aim then is to manipulate your transaction costs for decisions. Specifically, you want to minimize your transaction costs for good decisions while increasing the transaction costs for bad decisions. You want to encourage good decisions, such as eating healthy or managing your time, by making them easier for you so that they "cost" less. Meanwhile, flip the tables and make bad habits, like being disorganized, having poor time management, and procrastinating, too expensive to entertain.

How do you manipulate transaction costs in this way?

In simpler terms, if you want to encourage good decisions, you must make it easy—almost the default option if possible. For instance, if you want to practice an instrument more, what are the costs involved there that you can control? You can make it easier to practice your instrument by leaving it on your desk, making clear notes as to what to practice, giving yourself fun goals, and clearing time in your schedule every day to practice. You are making it easy to make the decision that is optimal.

It requires a bit of upfront work, but when you set yourself up thusly, you will have lowered the transaction costs and made it easy to make a good decision whether your ego is depleted or not.

You can make poor decisions cost too much in a similar way. For instance, if you wanted to raise the transaction costs of eating poorly, you would remove all junk food from your house, only buy healthy snacks, put bottles of water everywhere around your workspace so you don't feel the angst of hunger, and learn healthy substitutes for fatty food options. You are making it easy to ignore the decision that is suboptimal.

If it helps, you can think of transaction costs as the amount of willpower you must exercise. Thus, the lower the transaction costs are in general, the more willpower you can conserve for the decisions that truly matter.

A major key to effective decision-making is to understand how decision fatigue will impact you. It's more than a folksy concept or an excuse for being lazy. Decision fatigue and ego depletion are very real. If the phrase "Okay, just pick one. I don't care anymore" is familiar, you've been through it.

Takeaways:

- The concept of ego depletion is important because it leads directly to decision fatigue. When you reach decision fatigue, your decisions become incredibly suboptimal because you will either become paralyzed or make a rash, unresearched decision.
- How can you preemptively deal with the effects of ego depletion and willpower fatigue? You can time your decisions wisely such that they made only when rested, you can categorize the trivial daily decisions you have and make sure to only allot a trivial amount of time to them, you can treat yourself like an athlete and make sure you are mentally tapering off in preparation of big decisions, you can give yourself more time than is necessary to reduce the role of stress and anxiety, and you can also work on manipulating your

transaction costs to make good decisions more of a default option.

Chapter 3. The Six Hats Method and WRAP

Decision-making isn't necessarily a science, but you've seen at least a few methods that strive to put more thought and analysis into decisions.

We started the book by talking about what drives you on a deeper level. We are all driven by subconscious needs, and it's going to be better for you if you can make the subconscious just a little bit more conscious. That requires introspection aside from the act of actually making decisions.

This chapter is a more traditional way of thinking about decisions—in that we are seeking to analyze the factors present in insightful ways. These are mostly conscious factors, but they likely include angles and perspectives you've never considered. In a sense, they are templates for you to apply to your own unique situation. They take the information available and shine a different light onto it to aid your quest for optimal decisions.

The first of these such methods is the six hats method.

The Six Hats Method

It's one of my favorite decision-making methodologies because it is extremely thorough and focuses on what humans don't excel at—taking different perspectives. The six hats method presents you with a veritable checklist to run through while you try to make a decision, which ensures that all your bases are covered.

We've all heard the term that you must wear more than one hat. The six hats method was created by Edward de Bono, and as you might have guessed, it requires looking at a problem or decision from six separate perspectives by wearing six different hats.

Along with the hats themselves, an avatar that embodies the main purpose of each hat will make matters much clearer. It's like you are making a decision by committee, but all the roles are played by you.

The colors of the six hats are white, red, black, yellow, green, and blue. The colors are fairly inconsequential, and it's probably easier if you categorize them by the avatar. I'll go into each of them in depth.

"Tell me more. What does this mean, and where did you get that information?"

The white hat is Sherlock Holmes. This is the thinking and analytical hat. You are trying to gather as much information as possible by whatever means possible. Be observant and act like an information sponge. While you're at it, analyze your information and determine the gaps you have and what you can deduce from what you currently have. Dig deep, fill in the information gaps, and try to gather an understanding of what you really have in front of you.

You want to absorb as much of the available information as you can while also determining what you are missing to make a more informed and more perfect decision. The white hat is also where you should be resourceful about learning. As we discussed earlier, lack of information is one of the worst detriments to your decisions.

Make sure you are armed with information and you seek multiple perspectives and not let yourself be influenced by bias. You want an objective view at the entire landscape. Get out your magnifying glass and start sleuthing, Detective Holmes.

"And how does that make you feel? Why is that?"

The red hat is Sigmund Freud, the psychotherapist. This is your emotion hat. You are trying to determine how you feel about something and what your gut tells you. Those are not always the same emotion. Combined with the information you collected as Sherlock Holmes, this will already give you a more complete picture than you are used to.

You are asking how you feel about your options and why. Beyond the objective level, decisions affect us on an emotional level. You must account for that—happiness and unhappiness. Ask yourself what you find yourself leaning toward or avoiding and why that might be. You can also attempt to predict how others might react emotionally. Your actions might have consequences beyond your current understanding, and how people will feel is often different from how you think they will feel. What are the origins of your emotions toward each option, and are they reasonable or even relevant, for that matter? Often, our emotions aren't in the open, so when you can understand them better, you will understand your options better.

"I don't know. I have my doubts. What about X? Will Y really happen that way?"

The black hat is Eeyore, the morose donkey from *Winnie the Pooh*. If you don't know who that is, you can imagine the black hat to be the ultimate depressed pessimistic that never believes anything will work out. Indeed, the purpose of the black hat is to attempt to poke holes in everything and to try to account for everything that can go wrong. They are skeptics who always look on the darker side of life.

They believe in *Murphy's Law*: everything that can go wrong *will* go wrong. This is a hat most people never wear because they are afraid to look at their decisions, or reasoning, from a critical point of view. On some level, it probably indicates recognition that their views fall apart under deeper scrutiny, but that is exactly why it's so important to wear the black hat.

It's essentially planning for failure and the worst-case scenario. Planning for success is easy and instantaneous, but what happens when things don't work out and you have to put out fires? How would you plan differently if you thought there was a high probability of failure?

You change your approach, look for alternatives, and create contingency plans to account for everything. This is the type of analysis that leads to better planning and decisions because you can objectively take into account what is good and what is not. Wearing your black hat makes your plans tougher and stronger over the long haul, though it can be exhausting to continually reject positivity and hopefulness.

"It's going to be so great when this all comes together. Just imagine how you'll feel."

The yellow hat is the cheerleader. It is the opposite of the black hat—you are now thinking positivity and optimistically. This is a motivating hat that allows you to feel good about your decision and the value of putting all the work into it. This is where you turn dark clouds into a silver lining.

It also allows you to project into the future and imagine the opportunities that come along with it. If this decision goes well, what else will follow? Where do optimistic projections place you, and what is necessary for you to reach them?

Belief in yourself is still one of the concepts that fuels achievement and motivation, so it's important to be balanced with pessimism and nitpicking flaws.

"Call me crazy, but what if we completely change X and try Y?"

The green hat is Pablo Picasso, the famous artist. This hat is for creativity. When you wear this hat, you want to think outside the box and come up with creative perspectives, angles, and solutions to whatever you are facing. It can be as simple as pretending that your current leading option is unavailable and having to figure out what you can do instead. You have to deviate from the current options and discover other ways of solving your problem.

Brainstorming is the name of the game here. No judgment or criticism is allowed when you are wearing this hat because you want to generate as many ideas as possible. You can always curate them later, but the more solutions you can think of, no matter how zany or ineffective, there will always be something you can learn or apply from them.

This is also a hat of open-mindedness and not being stuck in one track of thinking, which can be dangerous if you refuse to alter your course in the face of hardships.

"Now, now, children. Everyone will have their turn to be heard."

The blue hat is Henry Ford, founder of Ford Motor Company and inventor of the modern assembly line. The blue hat is all about coordinating and creating a system to integrate all the information you obtained from the other hats. You can also look at this hat as the CEO hat: you are in charge of making things happen and putting things in place, though not necessarily in charge of creating anything by yourself.

You are in charge of weighing how heavily each hat should be considered and what factors you must take into account when integrating the information. The CEO knows the context the best, so the input from each different hat is synthesized and weighed based on personal priorities and the situation at hand. You are the ultimate decider.

Now that you know how each hat works, it's time to illustrate how they all work together. Let's suppose you are considering buying a new house.

Wearing the white Sherlock hat, you would examine all the information you have about the current market. That wouldn't be enough, so you would conduct far more independent research on the economy and market trends and come up with a clear sense of how much it will cost you, where you will live in the meantime, and if you are okay with the long-term tradeoff.

You would want prices on everything, data on past prices, predictions on future prices, and the other benefits and drawbacks to living in the new house. Then you'd take all that data and compare it to your current living situation, as well as to other houses in the area.

Wearing the red Freud hat, you would introspect and determine how you feel about the new house emotionally and intuitively. Will it make you happy regardless of the cost? What does your gut tell you? Money certainly can't buy happiness, but it can set the stage for it. Is the new house going to help with that? Are you drained by this process or energized by it? Recall that the red hat suggests you think about the emotional impact your decision will have.

Wearing the pessimistic Eeyore black hat, you would try to plan for the worst-case scenario for before and after you buy this new house—for example, if the market tanks and the house drops in value by half or if you lose your job and have to relocate to a new city far away from your new house. In a darker turn, you might lose your job and not be able to find a new one, meaning you'd be saddled with a mortgage that you can't pay.

What other factors inside or outside of your control might make purchasing a new house a terrible decision? The construction might be faulty, the previous owner might have lied to you, and the neighbors might be horrible. Plan for them so you can account for them.

Wearing the optimistic cheerleader yellow hat, what is the best-case scenario for purchasing a new house and how will that affect and benefit your life? Perhaps the house will increase twofold in value in the next three years, and perhaps you will be able to sell it for a huge profit while still living in the area. It might be a house for your family, so you'll feel stable and secure while in a good school district. Do these outweigh any potential negatives?

Despite all the problems for the new house, it might be nicer than anything you've ever lived in, and it represents a dream come true for you. Worst-case scenario, you can always rent a room to your cousin.

Wearing the Picasso green hat of creativity, you can think of additional ways to solve your problem of wanting to live in a new place. For example, would you sleep on a friend's couch to see if you need a big house? Rent a monthly house in the area first before committing to purchasing? Put in a new stove in your current house and find you won't have to move? What other areas of the city do you want to explore and live in? How else can you invest the money in a safe and smart way? Do you actually want to live in a new home, or do you have other desires?

When you get to the blue Henry Ford hat, your job is to sort through all the information you've uncovered, try to decide what is really important, and use it to make the most informed decision of your life. Perhaps you've decided that the money is simply too tight for a new house, and what you really wanted was to have a nicer kitchen. Or perhaps you've found that the housing market is at an all-time low, so even if you are low on money, it would be one of the best financial decisions to immediately take the leap.

The point of the six hats method is to take a deep dive into a particular perspective and temporarily tune everything else out. Give it free reign and reject all opposition to it for the time being. That's just about the only way you will be able to make a compelling argument for something that you don't wholeheartedly believe in at first. You want to embody the hat you currently wear and have a debate with yourself, moderated by the blue hat.

The hats represent your interests. You'll be able to see clearly which interests of yours you have focused on in the past. They might be interests that you don't prioritize as much as others, but they are your interests regardless. It's all a process to make sure that your top interests win out in the end (if they deserve to).

It's a WRAP

The other decision methodology comes from a formidable pair of brothers, Chip and Dan Heath, who are professors at Stanford University and Duke University, respectively. It is known as the WRAP methodology, which is an acronym that we'll dive into shortly.

The purpose of the WRAP approach is to make better decisions by focusing on often overlooked factors that tend to have far bigger implications that what we might traditionally look at. It's also what we've sought to do with the checklists and descriptions of subconscious influencers throughout the book.

WRAP works on the assumption that we are always trying to make decisions and generally think with the least amount of work possible.

Unfortunately, this is more due to necessity and circumstance—why do more in-depth thinking and analysis when we don't have to and have other things to get to?

Well, we usually have to, which means we take mental shortcuts that often put us onto the wrong path. What do these shortcuts look like? They are countless.

- Imperfect or incomplete information
- Seeing a pattern or causation where there is none
- Influence by a strong emotion
- Overconfidence
- Fatigue
- Laziness
- Incorrect underlying assumptions or beliefs

Even if you're in a rush, WRAP makes you look past those shortcuts and do the work, so to speak, in four thorough steps. WRAP stands for the following:

1. Widen your options.

2. Reality-test your assumptions.
3. Attain distance.
4. Prepare to be wrong.

This stands in stark contrast to most people's decision-making methodology, which might consist of the following (at most):

1. Look at most available options.
2. Select an option.
3. Cross your fingers and hope for the best.

Widen Your Options. This is the first step because most people only settle for options that are immediately available and right in front of their faces. They only consider the low-hanging fruit and think in conventional terms, dismissing other approaches for arbitrary reasons.

When you widen and expand the set of options you have, you immediately increase the chances of an optimal decision. This is easier said than done, because we usually think in black and white terms: yes or no, X or

Y. We don't consider the possibility that the answer or decision can be *maybe* or Z.

Sometimes just below the surface lies another level of options that you would never have seen if you didn't dive in, kick up the dust, and take a serious look. Even adding one alternative choice will benefit you greatly and provide additional insight into your decision.

Of course, this comes with the negative effect of prolonging a process and increasing inefficiency, but if you are looking for the absolute best option, it's imperative to widen your options.

For example, what options do you have when you want to increase a company's revenue? You can look at the hard assets like training better salesmen, reducing overhead, and downsizing. These are the low-hanging fruit— what other options do you have to increase revenue? What if you looked at how happy your salesmen were, how you could motivate them better, where are you losing money in your vendor contracts, or what sources of needless spending the company engages in? The list is endless.

These are the types of options you need to generate before making a decision. You might not find the very best one, but you are likely to find options that will still greatly impact your bottom line, whatever it may be.

Reality-Test Your Assumptions. What does this mean? It means to put your options to the test and go through the motions of what obstacles your options will encounter. Really think through what the future would look like and try to imagine every little detail. Often our options are plagued by confirmation bias and hubris, which means you won't be able to consider them objectively if you become attached to them. That's natural, and that's why it's necessary to go through this step.

It puts your decision on stage in front of an audience full of skeptics, and the skeptics will be lobbing difficult questions and asking you to answer them. They will force you to go through every step and explain in painstaking detail about what will happen next. When airplane manufacturers make sure their airplanes are ready for flight, they put the planes through a rigorous process known as stress testing, which includes flexing the wings and running the plane through physical and electric hardships to make sure that it holds up.

Reality-testing is no different.

Allow others to try to find holes in your option, and realize if you are trying to defend yourself based on rationalizations or based on actual facts and evidence. Of course, you may not have the option of the peanut gallery to ask you questions, so you have to train yourself to ask better questions and mentally visualize each step more consistently.

Let's stay with the example we used earlier of increasing a company's revenue. How might you reality-test your options here? Focus on one at a time and playing them out to their logical conclusion. Go through each step in the process and don't gloss over potential problems by saying, "Oh, we'll take care of that when it comes, no problem."

If you decide to focus on training your salesmen to be more effective and persuasive, you need to look at the costs involved in that and how it will play out in the next year or two, as training is a longer-term process. Then you must act like its biggest critic and ask how much increased revenue you will see, whether it's worth it, if the salesmen are capable of it, how it compares to the other options, when you can expect revenue to increase, how it can be done less expensively, and so on. Start with the five journalistic questions of who, what, when, where, and why, and move on from there.

Remember, you win if you find a flaw. If you don't find any, you still win.

Attain Distance. Attaining distance from your option means that you must take a moment and remove yourself from the process. Otherwise, you run the risk of letting your sense of triumph and short-term emotional attachment to an option color your decision.

Emotion can seep into any phase of the WRAP process and completely overpower your sense of logic and analysis. When you find confirmation and validation for your option, its natural to fall into a spiral of confidence and happiness. This is dangerous without distance.

In other words, take some time to sit on your decision. Sleep on it if necessary. Return after some psychological and mental distance to see if your justifications and reasoning still make sense. They might not.

If you've written anything in your life, you might be familiar with this phenomenon. You write something on Monday and it feels like the next Charles Dickens novel. You put it aside and bask in your triumph. When you reread it again the next Monday, you may find that it is barely intelligible. That's the power of distance.

Prepare to Be Wrong. Preparing to be wrong isn't assuming that you will be wrong. It's actually a thought exercise in finding alternate options and evaluating how effective they are.

If you succeed with your option, that's great, but success isn't really the scenario we need to plan for. Things are easy when we find success. We need to plan for when things go wrong or not as planned, because that's when we need to come up with a new approach and discover if your options are as good as you think.

In other words, prepare to be wrong by creating a Plan B and possibly Plan C, if possible. No matter how certain you are, unpredictability is still a possibility. Plan so that you can hit the ground running instead of panicking whenever you see a small wrench in your plans. You might even begin your decisions by opting for the best Plan B.

To increase a company's revenue, you might have decided that training your salespeople better is the unquestioned best choice. You've done the reality test and thought through the possibilities. However, what if it doesn't work on account on something you can't possibly control or foresee?

You would want to know what Plan B and Plan C are and how you can move into those seamlessly. What are the first steps so that you don't waste any time scrambling if Plan A falls short? What is going to get you closer to your goal while giving up the smallest cost? Preparing to be wrong is all about how you can adapt to adversity.

The WRAP process and the six hats method may seem like a lot of work, but all they are doing is uncovering your blind spots. If you are making decisions flying by the seat of your pants and relying upon your laser-sharp instinct, that's only going to lead to good decisions out of luck. And that's not a habit you want to continue.

Takeaways:

- Most of us engage in very little with regards

to our decisions. A pros and cons list, perhaps. But this still leaves us victims of your blind spots.

- The six hats method of decision-making implores you to view a fork in the road from six distinct different perspectives. Typically these are represented by colors, but avatars are more illustrative. The six different perspectives to consider are Sherlock Holmes (gather information), Sigmund Freud (emotions), Eeyore the donkey (pessimist), a cheerleader (optimist), Pablo Picasso (creativity), and Henry Ford (information synthesis).

- The WRAP method was devised to specifically address blind spots. WRAP stands for widen your options, reality-test, attain distance, and prepare to be wrong. As you can see, these are not typical ways to approach a decision, though they can serve you well because they represent what is likelier to happen in the real world.

Chapter 4. Making Calculations

One of the simplest and easiest ways we make decisions is through a pros and cons list. For some, it's the first instinct because it allows us to get our thoughts down onto paper regarding a big decision. Unlike other methods we'll talk about in this book, this chapter is about detailed cost-benefit analyses. Here, we try to identify what matters and quantify them, which can help lead to a better-informed decision.

We operate on a simple black and white standard of *more is better*. There is no gray area after the math is done.

Some of us might never even make it to this point, but the pros and cons list is often the first step for people who are really contemplating a tough choice.

Beyond Pros and Cons

The first method is to write a simple pros and cons list with a twist. This is actually a method American founding father Benjamin Franklin described in a letter dispensing advice on how to make intelligent decisions.

The typical pros and cons list works by listing what you would gain from a choice in one column and what you would lose from the decision in another column. Here's what a list might look like if you're contemplating eating pizza:

Pros: It's tasty, you satisfy cravings, you love cheese, it's in a nice part of the city, it's your cheat day, you'll feel happier after, you can save money

Cons: You are still trying to lose weight, you don't need it, you will binge on soda, too, you will feel gassy afterward

It's short and effective and helps you organize all the thoughts running through your head. You can categorize factors as simply positive or negative and see which side appears to have more than the other. It allows you to visually see your arguments instead of debating them mentally.

It gives you a way to analyze your choices based on what appears to be important. It also introduces the idea that you are making a decision about changing the status quo or not, which accurately reflects what you are actually deciding about. Make sure you are asking the right question.

Pros and cons lists highlight the importance of understanding what issues you face in making decisions. However, basic pros and cons lists break down in the face of more complex decisions than eating pizza or not. What if you are trying to analyze whether you should move to a new city or not?

What if you are trying to make a decision at work that has the potential to bring in two million in revenue—or not?

A simple pros and cons list breaks down in these situations because every factor appears to be the same and only counts for one. In other words, let's suppose you have a pro of making two million and a con of an increased commute by ten minutes. They obviously aren't equal in significance or magnitude, but in a simple pros and cons list, they would be because they take up the same amount of space: one line on a sheet of paper.

There's got to be a better way. How can we improve your old-fashioned pros and cons lists to be more effective and informative? We can do it by *quantifying* them. It can work in a few ways.

You'll still have a column each for positives and negatives that would occur if you engage in an action, but you will be assigning values on a scale of 0–10 to each argument that represents how important it is to you. For the previous example of revenue versus commute time, you would assign the revenue a value of 10, where the commute time might have a value of 1.5. The higher the score, the more important it is to you.

There are a couple of ways to look at the results. The first one is to simply decide in favor of whichever side's values add up to be higher. This is black and white. For example, if your pros add up to be 74 and your cons add up to 75, you would choose in favor of the con and not partake in the act. This is a straightforward and direct approach, but many people will have difficulty with it if the results are close. Indeed, if you are choosing between moving to a new city versus staying put, perhaps you should have overwhelming reasons and evidence to do so; otherwise, there are not enough compelling reasons.

In this case, the second way to look at the results is to only act if the value of the pros list comes to be twice the value of the cons side. For example, if your pros add up to 90 but your cons add up to 70, you probably shouldn't act, because there isn't strong enough reason to break your inertia and uproot yourself from the status quo. It's not worth it to expend the effort into learning new tasks and changing your lifestyle for a marginal gain of 20 value points, so to speak. This is an approach that favors the status quo because it realizes that motion is not always progress; sometimes it is just wasted effort.

The second method is what I personally prefer because I, like many people, am lazy. I don't want to do something that will require extra effort and work if it doesn't result in a significant gain for me.

If there isn't a clear, powerful reason for me to do something, why do it? In this way, I try to make decisions as binary as possible. Is there a powerful reason that significantly overrides the negatives? If so, let it fly. If not, don't waste your effort unless you are seeking change for change's sake.

There are multiple standards of interpreting the results that your quantified pros and cons list produces: whichever is greater, if the pros side is twice as large as the cons, or any other arbitrary number differential that appeals to you. What matters is you are simultaneously finding your priorities as you assign values to everything.

There are also multiple ways to quantify the lists themselves. Instead of how important something might be to you, you can assign values based on the following:

- How much money it saves
- How much time it saves
- How close it gets you to a certain goal
- How happy it makes you
- How annoyed it makes you
- How much your significant other will care about it

This allows you to adapt your pros and cons list to the specifics of your situation, which is good practice in general. If you use generalized or abstract pros and cons arguments that are irrelevant to your situation or worldview, you will get an answer that doesn't accurately reflect your situation.

For example, suppose you are trying to decide whether to buy a new car or stick with the same car you've had for the last five years. Let's list the pros and cons quantified with how important the factor is to my happiness.

Pros:
- Feel better about self, 6
- Impress women more easily, 8
- Better mileage on commute, 3
- More comfortable leather, 8
- Better sound system, 8

Cons:
- Cost, 9
- Don't need it, 7
- Bad buying time right now, 8
- Would need to take a loan from parents, 6
- Higher insurance, 7

It's the act of going through and honestly assigning values to everything that also lets you find what is important to you. Some people might want a car because they figure it will be better for their commute, but when they honestly assess themselves, it might be just because they enjoy the ego boost a fancy car provides on a daily basis. And that's okay. Understanding what you're basing your decisions on is as important as the factors themselves.

Second, if you can understand what factors are important in your decisions, it allows you to see what you can address independently of the big decision itself. In this example, it appears that independent of the new car, the sound system and the leather seats appear to be very important. Instead of going all in on a new car, you can just address what bothers you about the current car and make a more efficient decision.

The last important factor in better, quantified pros and cons lists is to be aware of which factors are fixed and which are subject to change in the future. Your world may not be the same next year as it is today, much less tomorrow. The things on your list may change for better or worse. However, only some of those will change, while others are more or less static for all time. This is something to keep in mind because it means a con may not always be a con and a pro may not always be a pro. How much deviation are you willing to factor in and accept as time goes on?

For example, do you expect that you will always want a better sound system, or is that something that is in your mind right now because of a new coworker's influence? Differentiate between what can and cannot be changed at all, and make sure you aren't going into a decision with the idea that factors *will* change. That's like marrying someone depending on the fact that they will undergo a sex change. It's putting the cart before the horse in a major way.

Hopefully this can change the way you fundamentally look at pros and cons lists. They can be as complex as you wish.

Force Field Analysis

Force Field Analysis (FFA) is another method of quantifying your decisions. It was created by Kurt Lewin in the 1940s, and he originally used it in his occupation as a social psychologist. Today, we use it for the purpose of making optimal decisions.

Even though the title is quite ambiguous and abstract-sounding, it's relatively simple. FFA works best when you are deciding between making a change and remaining in the status quo, and it looks at the forces that are *driving* the change versus the forces that are *resisting* the change. You can either decide to stay the course or switch things up.

So this method is not merely analyzing whether or not it is a smart decision; it is analyzing the likelihood of success and what it would take otherwise. This is a crucial element of taking action, because if you could know that your change, while a good idea, was never going to stick, then it would be pointless. It can and should influence your actions.

FFA depends on looking at *driving and resisting forces*. To boil it down, for you to take action and cause change, the driving forces must be made stronger or the resisting forces must be weakened in some way. This is similar to a criterion for the quantified pros and cons list—in order for action to be taken, there should be significant reason for change. FFA is best illustrated through an example.

The first step is to describe the change you want and contrast that to the status quo. For instance, you might want to institute a new and improved retirement plan at a company. There are many pros and cons to this, but remember, FFA measures how likely the plan is to succeed and be accepted.

The second step is to identify the forces that would *drive* the change. These can be anything you can think of that would make instituting a new retirement plan more likely to succeed and be well received. In this example, they can include unhappy workers, a declining economy, tax benefits, increased revenues, and company morale. These are the reasons your change may be successful.

The third step is to identify the forces that would resist the change. A good portion of these will always be the same, with factors such as inertia, laziness, fear, a lack of enthusiasm, and sticking to old conventions. But the other factors will be specific to the situation at hand—in this context, creating a new retirement plan: potential tax problems, government regulation, the expense of hiring accountants and lawyers, and gaining the approval of the board of directors. These are the obstacles that will stop your change dead in its tracks and make this decision useless.

The fourth step is to assign scores to each factor you named in the previous two steps. You want to assign a score of 1–5, weakest to strongest, based on how much influence the factor has on the change. You will be aggregating the scores for both the change factors and the resistance factors.

The fifth step is to take a step back and look at what you've got. You've essentially performed the FFA and you just have to analyze your results now. Remember, the question is whether or not you should be moving forward on the suggested change or stick with the status quo. Should you move forward with instituting a new and improved retirement plan at a company? Are your driving forces powerful enough to overcome the resisting forces? Which of the two forces will win?

As is, you may not have enough compelling reasons to believe that your change would be successful. That's when you need to change the equilibrium, if you're deadset on instituting that retirement plan. Changing the balance may involve strengthening driving forces, weakening resisting forces, or a combination of the two. It depends how determined you are to implement your change—but you now have a roadmap of what it will take to implement successfully and what obstacles you will face.

FFA is different from traditional decision-making models because it measures the success of the decision versus whether or not it is a beneficial decision. Coupled with the quantified pros and cons list, there are ways of satisfying the inner analyst to optimize your decisions.

Takeaways:

- A simple pros and cons list is a big step for many, but it is not the most effective tool without modification. A highly suggested modification is to quantify your pros and cons list, which is where you assign numeric values to each item to get a clear sense of what matters and what your priorities are. After compiling your two lists, you can choose to evaluate the sums in different manners, such as straight addition, or requiring a certain differential to take action.

- The Force Field Analysis method of decision-making is different than other methods because it is purely about whether or not you should make a change or stick with the status quo. It actually measures how successful your change should be by comparing driving and resisting factors. If you are dead set on leaving the status quo, then you can manipulate the factors by boosting the driving factors or decreasing the resisting factors.

Chapter 5. Mental Checklist

Continuing with the theme of different considerations in making decisions, this chapter presents more factors that have likely never crossed your mind and can make you happier through better selection.

Even though the objectives and factors in any decision are going to be different on any given day, there are still lines of thought you should apply to every one of them for an optimal decision that benefits you and doesn't actively hurt you.

If we are honest with ourselves, the reason we don't engage in this type of thinking is because we are lazy or we don't think we have to. We overrate our ability to make decisions in an odd sense of hubris. We think we should go with our gut or live on our instinct, but study after study has proven our sense of impulsive decisions to be fairly unreliable.

This will slow down your decisions, but it will give you additional templates you can use to make sure all of your bases are covered and you are making the best move for yourself in light of all the relevant factors.

The 10/10/10 Rule

The first part to incorporate into your mental checklist is the 10/10/10 rule.

The 10/10/10 rule is very straightforward and asks you to travel through time. When you are at a fork in the road, ask yourself how you will feel about the choice you make: 10 **minutes** from now, 10 **days** from now, and 10 **months** from now? Depending on the scope and context of the decision, you can make it longer or shorter terms in nature. Shorter periods of time correspond to decisions with smaller stakes and more immediate consequences, while longer periods of time correspond with larger stakes and more delayed consequences.

If you want to debate eating a slice of pizza, you might do 10 minutes, 10 hours, and 10 days. You'd find that eating a pizza or hamburger in the moment really doesn't affect your life very much in any timeline. If you want to decide what city to move to, you can use 10 weeks, 10 months, and then 10 years in the future. You can see how your decisions can greatly impact your life if you view it through the lens of the future.

Travel through time and explore the consequences in each scenario. The 10/10/10 rule begs you to ask your future self about the decisions and approaches you make today. Make sure you are happy with the outcomes of each timeline you think about; if you aren't, is it actually a wise decision? Likewise, if you aren't happy with all of the outcomes, then are you willing to take on that informed risk?

The rule lays out consequences and aftereffects in a very real and tangible manner and forces you to step back from your immediate emotion or impulse about a course of action or decision. It creates a mindset in which you articulate your short- and long-term goals before moving toward them. How do they play out and what ripple effects will they have?

The 10/10/10 rule impacts your range of choices because things that may seem important or easy to do now might not lead to either the small or big goals you want for the future. They might actually lead nowhere and just waste your time if you think through the appropriate 10/10/10 time periods. You might find that they are detrimental in a longer time period, and you were seduced into taking a short-term profit for a long-term loss.

When you apply the 10/10/10 rule, you train your mind to look at long-term implications. It is just as important for you to train your mind to look at your options and see whether they will advance you toward achieving your bigger goals. At the very least, you get a feel for the overall impact of the choice in front of you and whether it furthers your ultimate success or not.

It can impact the things you eat, the clothes you buy, the jobs you apply for, the people you spend time with, and obviously the business opportunities you wish to take advantage of.

This exercise highlights what is truly important and what is not so consequential to you. Remove impulse and temptation from your life, and let discipline propel you forward. The 10/10/10 rule also teaches you to analyze delayed gratification. You might feel great about a decision in 10 minutes, but you might feel terrible about it in 10 days.

Worldview

The second part of your mental checklist is literally a checklist of questions to ask yourself to make sure that you are actually making a wise choice for yourself. These questions make sure your decisions are aligned with your worldview, and they help you eliminate options right off the bat when you see that they don't fit in.

Again, these might not be entirely new concepts to you, but it's actually going through the motions that will set you apart from others and make your decisions as optimal as can be.

To make your decision, ask yourself these questions:

1. What are the main problems you are trying to solve? Can you solve them in any other way, either individually or together?
2. Do you have all the information necessary to make the best decision possible? If not, what information would you have in a perfect world?

3. Are any of the most important factors subject to change anytime soon? What realistic factors could instantly make you regret your decision?

4. What is the opportunity cost for this decision? In other words, what would you miss out on to take this current opportunity?

5. Does this get you closer to your overall pertinent goals? Or does it take you further away from them?

6. Are you making this decision out of a sense of duty and obligation or out of your actual free will?

When you get a sense of the answers to these questions, it becomes hard to lie to yourself or fool others into believing you. You run out of space to do something that isn't good for you when you articulate your motivations and reasoning. When you can "pass" all of these questions, it becomes clear that you are making the decision for yourself, because you want to, and with a clear purpose.

Going through this part of the checklist is like going through a mini polygraph (the lie detector test) test. It cuts through the chatter and makes clear what you want, even if it wasn't clear to you beforehand.

Boundaries

The third part of the mental checklist for optimal decisions is to set subjective boundaries for your decisions. It's important to set these beforehand, because when you're in the heat of the moment, it's very difficult to think clearly and objectively.

When you set them beforehand, as you can do while reading this chapter, you can control your impulses and emotional reactions better. You can think of boundaries as rules and hard guidelines for you to abide by. They help you limit your choices and can even allow you to come to a decision through a process of elimination.

For example, if you go on a shopping trip, you might decide on a spending limit. You can't buy a jacket for over $100, or you can't spend over $200 total for the day. This is a specific metric that you can't exceed under any circumstances. It allows you to quickly eliminate options because you're simply limited to things under a certain amount. It narrows your scope based on predetermined requirements. Specific limits can help reduce your options because you can also set a limit on the number of options you even consider or a time limit on how long you have until you pull the trigger.

Another boundary is to name deal breakers or options that you will never consider based on a trait or characteristic. For example, if a car has a safety rating below a certain number, it's out of the question for you. Another example is to not visit cities that drop below a certain temperature. Deal breakers help you focus on what you prioritize and immediately avoid things you don't to save time.

A final type of boundary to help streamline your decision-making is to apply criteria for your decisions. *I will only do it if it is X.*

Again, these are decided on beforehand so you aren't influenced by a lack of willpower or emotion. You can think of these as the opposite of deal breakers. If an option possesses this trait or characteristic, it is automatically your choice.

For example, you might only choose the best camera on the market below $200. It would be your one trait to look for, and it would rule out every camera except two or three. At the very least, this excludes all of the bad options and leaves you a small subset that you would probably be happy with. At this point, you might even be able to pick randomly after applying one of these boundaries.

Another example is to only spend time pursuing a sales lead if it will be worth over $5,000 so you aren't wasting your time on something that would not amount to much. You could also only watch movies in theaters that have a certain ranking and ignore all others that fall below it. Finally, you could decide to not spend over $15 per restaurant meal, which would severely limit your choices.

Not only does this make your life easier by preemptively making sure your decisions fit into your life, but it also serves to limit decision fatigue. Recall that the ability to make decisions is not infinite and has a limited capacity due to the consumption of glucose in your brain. When you can apply these filters to many aspects of your life, especially trivial everyday decisions, you are able to save your mental resources for what really matters.

Satisficing

The next part of your mental checklist is to ask whether you are embodying this unfamiliar word or not. The word *satisfice* is a combination of the words *satisfy* and *suffice*. It's a term that Herbert Simon coined in the 1950s, and it represents what we should shoot for rather than something that is guaranteed to optimize and maximize our happiness.

Generally, people can be split into those two categories: those who seek to satisfice a decision and those who seek to maximize a decision.

Let's suppose that you are shopping for a new bike. The maximizer would devote hours to researching their decision and evaluating as many options as possible. They would want to get the best one possible for their purposes and want to leave no stone unturned. They want 100% satisfaction, despite the law of diminishing returns and the Pareto principle, which would warn against such measures.

By contrast, the safisficer is just shooting to be satisfied and for an option that suffices for their purposes. They want something that works well enough to make them satisfied and pleased but not overjoyed or ecstatic. They aim for *good enough* and stop once they find that.

These are very different scales, and for this reason, studies have shown that satisficers tend to be happier with their decisions while maximizers tend to keep agonizing and thinking about greener pastures after their decisions.

Maximization represents a conundrum in our modern age, because while it is more possible than at any point in human history to get exactly what you want, there is also the paradox of choice, which makes it impossible to be satisfied. On a practical matter, there are few decisions where we should strive to maximize our value. Therefore, put forth proportional effort and just make a choice already.

Most of the time, you simply want something that is reliable and works. Suppose you are in a grocery store and you are trying to pick out the type of peanut butter you want. What should you shoot for here? Satisficing or maximizing? The same type of thinking should apply to 99% of our daily decisions.

Otherwise, we are constantly overwhelmed and waste our mental bandwidth on maximizing where it doesn't matter and where there are massive diminishing returns. Whatever net benefit the most optimal type of peanut butter brings to your life is likely not worth the extra effort it took to find it.

It's unlikely that you're going to run to this chapter whenever you hit a fork in the road, but hopefully one or two lessons stick and you are able to make great decisions suited for you and no one else.

Takeaways:

- We are always battling our laziness in all aspects of life. With decisions, implementing a simple checklist of sorts can help.
- First, travel into the future with the 10/10/10 rule. This implores you to consider three different timelines in the future and how you'll feel about your decisions at those three points. Ideally, you want all three timelines to be positive; if not, can you live with the informed decision that one timeline might be negative or detrimental?

- Another mental check-in is to examine whether or not your options are in line with your worldview, and this is accomplished by asking a series of questions that both alleviate you of your blind spots and make clear the reasons you have for engaging in certain actions.

- Setting your own arbitrary boundaries can help with decisions because they narrow your options. You can set limits and use deal breakers or requirements—they all work to clarify your intentions and work more quickly.

- Are you satisficing or unknowingly trying to maximize every decision you make? Ninety-nine percent of daily decisions don't require maximization and suffer greatly from the law of diminishing returns. Satisficing, a combination of satisfaction and sufficing, is the key.

Chapter 6. Decision Traps

In a previous chapter, we touched upon two of the biggest indicators of intelligent decision-making: (1) understanding and working around decision fatigue and (2) avoiding stress and anxiety.

As if that wasn't enough, there are also literally hundreds of decisions traps, or cognitive biases, that can influence how you view a decision. Where the previous chapters were about you and your own filters, cognitive biases are specific flaws in logic or emotion that influence how you process the information right in front of your face. Information that could be plainly obvious to someone else might drive you in the opposite direction because of one of these cognitive decision biases.

The next two chapters might seem very obvious and familiar to you, and that's because you have probably fallen victim to their contents in the past. And you'd probably continue to fall victim to them in the future if they weren't pointed out to you.

Cognitive biases represent flaws in human thinking, whether logical or emotional in nature. They are conclusions that we leap to in the absence of, and sometimes in the face of, evidence that says otherwise. You can also think of them as a mental shortcut that seems to make sense at the time but falls apart under deeper scrutiny.

That said, it's very rare that we encounter such scrutiny, so most of us never realize we engage in these biases—and our decision quality suffers for it. They are a bit more complex than simply requiring more information. These are some of the ways our brains are fooled in everyday life.

For the purposes of illustration, I will be using the same example throughout the chapter: deciding between purchasing an expensive, brand-new car and a beat-up older car.

Preferring Simplicity

The first cognitive bias is that humans tend to prefer simplicity. In fact, we believe that something is more accurate the simpler it is. By contrast, we also distrust more complex things. We trust them less and we even become suspicious of them because we feel that decisions should be simple and straightforward. Some decisions *can* be direct, but most of life cannot be reduced to a single question.

In our example, buying a shiny new car is the simple solution. We can trust that it's new, we can see the mileage, and we know it hasn't been crashed before by some shady past owner. We seemingly know what we are getting. We sign, we buy, and we take the car off the lot. It doesn't get simpler than that.

By contrast, buying an older, used car has exponentially more moving parts—moving parts that could go wrong and that might not be in sync with each other. There are too many factors outside of our control that we aren't able to judge accurately. We always have a sense of suspicion and distrust when buying a used car because we never know how the car has been treated and if we are being told the entire truth.

We prefer simplicity in all walks of life, and that means the decisions that seem the simplest or have the fewest number of moving parts are almost always going to be preferred. They feel more trustworthy, like everything is transparent.

This also implies another aspect of what we prefer—we prefer things that we understand easily and immediately. If we can't, then it's as though there is a logical disconnect and something is being hidden—never mind the fact that many concepts cannot be broken down in such a fashion, but that's why this is a cognitive bias.

Studies have dubbed this *cognitive fluency*—how easily information is digested and understood. If information is easier and more closely resembles a model you already understand and can make a comparison to, it will feel familiar and fluent as a result. For example, there is a science to branding and marketing such that studies have found easily pronounceable names and reproducible logos perform far better than others. It's the power of simplicity.

We would love to quickly be able to ascertain the major points of competing decisions, and if we can't, then we mentally write off the more complex version. Just because something is simpler at first glance doesn't mean you should fall for the chance to reduce your due diligence. Sometimes simplicity *is* better, but by itself it means nothing.

Relying on Contrast

This cognitive bias can be seen very prominently in our example of buying cars. It's the error of being swayed by relative values. It occurs frequently when you make a comparison to something that doesn't matter yet creates a large contrast, which is not always the metric you should actually be considering.

Let's say the expensive new car you are looking at has a sticker price of $50,000. The used car is only $10,000. However, the new car is currently discounted from the original price of $90,000.

By simply introducing the relative discount, that sure makes it more attractive, doesn't it? Sometimes we will get caught in this trap of perceived value. It sounds like a good deal to get a $90,000 car for almost half off, but that assumes that the car is actually worth $90,000 and that $50,000 is also a fair price. By introducing the comparison to the number that isn't exactly relevant, one might actually feel that they're getting a steal at $50,000.

However, this isn't considering the car on its own merits or its own absolute value. This is considering it only in comparison to something it shouldn't be compared to: a relative value which makes it appear attractive.

You are stuck on a fundamental misunderstanding of comparisons, not wanting to miss out on something versus evaluating something in a vacuum by itself. Life doesn't operate in a vacuum, but it's important to keep your focus on the factors that actually matter in your decisions.

In this example, the best course of action would be to judge if the car is actually worth $50,000, despite how much of a discount the price represents. Then you can compare the absolute value of both the new and old cars at their respective price points to make a much better decision that is free of cognitive bias.

Otherwise, you just might be fooled into caring about something that is wholly irrelevant to what you are trying to accomplish. When battling the reliance on comparison cognitive bias, try to strip away the fancy trappings and focus on only one factor: the absolute, objective value.

Avoid All Loss

We hate to lose things.

In fact, we hate to lose things so much that we often would rather not lose anything as opposed to gain a lot. This is referred to as loss aversion, and it perfectly encapsulates people's strong tendency to prefer avoiding loss as opposed to acquiring gains. We build our decisions around the irrational desire to prevent loss, even when it doesn't benefit us very much.

Even if there is a net negative effect from a decision to avoid loss, it psychologically *feels* better than a net positive gain. Emotions are not always useful in high decision quality.

Studies by Kahneman and Tversky showed that the motivation, and thus decisional influencing, of avoiding losses are twice as powerful as acquiring a gain. If your number one priority in decisions is to avoid loss, then what happens to the rest of the considerations, which are often more relevant and important? Out the window.

How does this fit into our example of dueling cars, one used and one new? A buyer will buy from whichever salesman is able to make the buyer feel like they own the car as quickly as possible—by putting them in the car, referring to it as theirs, signing papers, or making them otherwise feel emotionally attached. The salesman could even give the car to someone for a 30-day free trial period, which would really cement the decision for the buyer. This creates the possibility for the feeling of loss we so wish to avoid.

Why is this? When someone gets familiar with a concept or object, especially in as tangible of a way as a 30-day trial, they grow ownership. Only when you have ownership and attachment does the possibility of loss begin to matter. People usually react with irrational rage over even threatened losses. The act of mentally hearing "It's yours, and I'm taking it away" has a greater effect than hearing "It's here, and I'm taking it away."

How do you think you might react if you thought you had bought the car, only to have it taken away based on a legal technicality? It would be akin to physical pain to part with something you feel is yours.

Loss aversion is a powerful motivation for your decisions, and it causes people to ignore gains to prevent losses, playing it safe in a sense when it doesn't actually make sense.

For instance, a 2013 study by Cullen et al. found that first giving someone a reward and then threatening to take it away as a penalty was a far better motivational tool than handing out a reward after achievement. The fear of losing something that was already yours, having it ripped from your fingers, was far more powerful.

The pain of losing, or losing out on, something is more salient and raw than the joy from gaining something. We suddenly feel that we have been robbed, which is a stronger emotion than receiving a gift. However, just because the emotions are so disproportionally weighted doesn't mean the path of loss aversion is smarter. The decisions are still equal; negative emotions just tend to take hold on us more strongly and blind us with fear or rage.

Scenario A: I give you $10, then flip a coin. If the coin lands on heads, I take the money back.

Scenario B: I flip a coin. If the coin is a heads, I give you $10. Which do you prefer? Scenario B is clearly more comfortable psychologically.

It's not to say that you should ignore negative consequence in decisions. It's only to caution and gain awareness that negative consequences have the ability to take root firmly in our brains and never let go. They can emotionally color our perspectives until all we want to do is avoid a slight amount of potential negativity at the expense of a sure positive gain.

Reduce Risk

Humans want to reduce risk whenever possible. This cognitive bias is about reducing the risk that you face in decisions—choosing the option that represents zero risk over something more lucrative that might have a slight increase in risk.

It is similar to the prior cognitive bias of loss aversion. We want to avoid losses because the emotion of loss is far more salient and painful than the emotion of gain, and it's the same with risk. The gut reaction of knowing you face a certain risk is far more powerful and convincing than the emotion for any marginal gain.

This is otherwise known as the zero-risk bias, and it's a cognitive bias that makes you prefer options where the primary goal is to eliminate one risk, where other options are actually better at reducing risk overall. That's an important distinction to make. We prefer one risk to be completely eliminated versus eliminating risk across the board.

A simple example of this is to imagine that there is a rowboat in the water with 10 leaks in the hull. The zero-risk bias would focus solely on plugging five of the holes completely and reducing the risk from those down to zero, while the option of using buckets to scoop the water out doesn't actually solve those problems but is overall better for the boat's survival.

In a 1983 study by Baron et al., a questionnaire was given regarding a hypothetical cleanup scenario involving sites X and Y. Site X had eight cases of cancer annually, while site Y had four cases annually. One might suppose that site X was more dangerous and required more cleanup.

The questionnaire gave two general cleanup options:

1. Reduce the cancer cases by six between the two sites.
2. Reduce the cancer cases by five between the two sites and completely eliminate the cases at site Y.

A significant portion, though not a majority, of subjects ranked option two as better, even though that yielded a worse result overall. That's the zero-risk bias—when people are willing to completely eliminate one risk at the expense of lower efficacy and outcomes. This speaks to how humans prefer to face problems—the fewer the better, even if the fewer are more powerful and harmful. There is a preference on juggling fewer balls because it *just* feels better and safer.

See how our emotional sides are getting the best of us yet again? You can imagine how this affects your decision quality and clouds your judgment. More problems are bad, yes, but the number of problems in itself is meaningless to the overall decision quality.

How does this play out in our new versus old car example? You would be basing your decisions on which car completely solves one problem for you and ignoring any other considerations or aspects. This might be good if you choose to focus on something like safety, but we are usually more fixated on things like horsepower or sleekness. What we ignore is the overall satisfaction we would gain from the car in favor of having a car that solves one issue sufficiently for us. Reducing risk sacrifices psychological comfort for good decisions.

Takeaways:

- Through no fault of our own, there are many ways our brains can actively fool us into suboptimal decisions.
- The first cognitive bias is a preference for simplicity and a distrust for complexity. Sadly, life isn't always so simple. This can lead us to prefer the simpler, more direct option over options that are perceived to be more complex and have hidden factors.

- The second cognitive bias is a reliance on contrast and relative value. This makes us susceptible to terrible decisions because relative value is meaningless to us—the only thing that should matter is objective and absolute value.
- The third cognitive bias is a tendency to avoid losses. The psychological harm of a loss is exponentially that of the psychological benefit of a gain—thus, we seek to avoid losses in decisions whenever possible, even when it is illogical.
- The fourth cognitive bias is a tendency to reduce risk. This is similar to the tendency to avoid losses. We act to reduce risk because it feels psychologically more comfortable and less stressful, despite usually being a poorer decision overall.

Chapter 7. Decision Traps Part Two

This is a continuation of the previous chapter on decision traps and cognitive biases. One can truly never learn enough ways that the mind is able to trick your conscious train of thought. It's probably more accurate to say that it's a minor miracle when we are able to stay on a straight path and ignore all the traps on the side.

We'll stick to the same example as before as well: the decision of buying an old car versus a new car to illustrate how we are tripped up by our own brains.

Unconscious Bias

Although each of these decision traps can be said to be unconscious, unconscious bias is a special label for a specific type of thinking that pervades our decisions.

Unconscious bias affects almost every area of our lives, especially the people in it and how we treat them. There are stereotypes about people we form without our conscious recognition. We all hold these beliefs and stereotypes based on social, racial, gender, or sexual forms, and any other type of categorization you can name. Unconscious bias is when we unknowingly allow these factors to figure into our decision calculus.

From a purely psychological standpoint, this is crucial for survival because instantly judging something can mean the difference between life and death. Is this a friendly dog or a hungry hyena running over to greet me? Does this person appear to be part of my tribe or a neighboring tribe that wants to conquer me?

This simple analysis takes into account a multitude of factors that would take a long time to articulate but that would be easy to feel based on stereotyping. We have evolved to process information quickly based on small contextual cues we have seen and experienced throughout our lives.

It helps survival, but we're no longer in that kind of danger on a daily basis. Unconscious bias is mostly detrimental to our lives these days because of the opportunities it causes us to miss and the decisions that we flub.

We might all like to think we are open-minded, but let's consider the car example. You are deciding between a new car and a used car. Perhaps, in your childhood, your parents bought a used car and it was always breaking down on them. Consequently, you have grown up with a hatred of used car salespeople because your family was wronged by one in the distant past.

You can't seem to bring yourself to buy a used car, and you keep inventing reasons and rationalizing why you need a new car instead. Are you able to pinpoint these feelings back to your childhood experiences? Are you even conscious about them, aside from a faint gut feeling of discomfort with used cars?

Probably not. But it hurts you nonetheless. We carry with us a lifetime of beliefs and ingrained thoughts that heavily influence both our worldview and the people in it. This in itself isn't a revelation, but the depths to which this affects us should be.

Among other things, we make decisions and prejudge people on things as trivial as their accent, the way they walk, their weight, and even their name. A 2004 study showed that identical résumés for job interviews had drastically different outcomes when there was a European name versus an African-American name. You can probably guess what the difference was.

No matter how unprejudiced you think you are, that only applies consciously. It's impossible to have the same opinion across the board of options and truly see things objectively in a vacuum. The only fix for this is a massive increase in exposure and interaction with different experiences and people, but who has the time for that? Thus, your decisions suffer as a result.

Confirmation Bias

This is the fancy way of saying we believe what we want to believe. Confirmation bias is the tendency to see, interpret, or seek information in a way to confirm our beliefs or preferences.

Ideally, all of our decisions would be based only on the evidence and facts. If you have an assumption, you test it and observe the evidence, and you adjust your assumption accordingly. However, it's hard to deny that whenever we have an idea stuck in our head, we often go out of our way to find a way to make it manifest. We're stubborn animals when we want to be, and it's a huge cognitive handicap.

Let's come back to our car dealerships. If you go into this process with the belief that only a certain brand of cars can be bought used, then you will see everything through that lens. It will serve as a given, or truth, for you. It's almost like evidence that sprang up from nothing but an errant thought in your head, or something you thought you read somewhere once.

You will search for information about that particular car brand and how it is indeed the only good used car. You'll ignore any evidence to the contrary as flawed or fake. You will interpret dubious information to be an exception or to actually prove your point in a backward way. If you believe you want to buy a Toyota, your research and analysis will only serve to confirm that belief.

This tells us two things. First, we want so much to be correct that we fool ourselves and ignore anything that tells us we're wrong. Apparently our egos need that on a daily basis even when we're not arguing with anyone else. Second, we just really, really hate being wrong, and we avoid that feeling by using the defense mechanism of confirmation bias. In either case, we are making suboptimal decisions.

A 1979 study by Snyder and Cantor even went so far as to show that confirmation bias affects not only how you interpret information, but also *what* you take in and absorb. Whatever the belief of the research participants was the information they were able to recall. They barely paid attention to information that contradicted their beliefs, as if it went in one ear and out the other. They literally created an echo chamber for themselves and maintained an environment where they were only surrounded by supporting facts and evidence. Someone else could read the same information and come away with an entirely different reality.

As you can see, confirmation bias is difficult to understand because its very nature is that it is not being detected. People are unaware they are ignoring contrary evidence; they just fixate on a particular stance or belief and commit to it prematurely.

Imagine that you decided when you were a teenager that you were destined to be a doctor, yet you discovered when you were in medical school that blood makes you faint. A strong confirmation bias would lead you to conclude that you happen to faint when blood is around because of other factors, and being around blood isn't even that important to being a doctor. Now, that doesn't sound right...

Gambler's Fallacy

The gambler's fallacy is the feeling that there are predictable patterns in what are actually random sets of events. It's when you give far too much credit to the amount of control you can exert over the universe.

For example, if you roll dice, you might feel that you should eventually roll a seven because it's time for it to happen. Never mind the fact that this is not statistically or probabilistically sound, you are attempting to create order in something that is impossible to have control over.

This is a cognitive bias that causes us to ignore the concept of probabilities and make a decision that makes zero logical sense. The gambler's fallacy is overall the notion that just because X happened, Y should happen, X shouldn't happen, or X should happen again. They are all, more often than not, independent of each other, and this should guide your decision-making to be less biased. There is no causation, and just like a gambler thinks "I'm due for a lucky hand at some point!" you will also think incorrectly.

For our car situation, the gambler's fallacy, or seeing patterns where there are none, makes a big difference. It will cause you to keep holding out for better models and lower prices on both the new and used car. This isn't something you can predict; you are simply trying to rely on a pattern that you've invented in your head that ultimately is incorrect. You have noticed what you perceived to be a pattern once, and the belief in that pattern is leading you down the wrong path. Each price that is associated with a new or used car for sale is independent of previous used car prices.

You are attempting to find logic and an explanation for a random series of events. There is no better illustration than how early mankind started to see entire scenes in the night sky in the form of constellations. The stars in the sky are certainly randomized, but there is the tendency to find patterns, make familiar, and put things into contexts we already know. Basing decisions only on verifiable evidence is what can put a stop to this cognitive bias.

Rosy Retrospection

This is the tendency toward having far fonder memories than what actually occurred. The name comes from the saying of seeing events through rose-colored glasses.

We have the tendency to remember the past in terms of positivity. Why?

There are many possibilities. We consciously want to make ourselves feel better about our experiences and make it feel like we didn't waste our time. Because we want to be able to say that we're having fun and appear positive in front of other people. Because we subconsciously want to defend our sense of self and our actions.

A study in 1992 by Robert Sutton surveyed subjects who visited Disneyland and found that their actual experience was actually tiring, irritable, and expensive. Their expectations were not met, and some even felt like they had wasted their time. However, when the same subjects were surveyed after the trip to Disneyland, they universally reported the trip being more enjoyable and fun than they had in the moment. It was as if they had selective memory and chose to bypass encoding the negative moments into their brains and only focused on the positive.

What's interesting is that even though people tend to remember the positives of their experiences, research has shown that negative memories are actually more impactful and powerful. A 2001 study by John Cacioppo found that the brain has substantially greater activity in response to negative stimuli versus positive stimuli.

What does this all mean? Our decisions are constantly taken hostage by our faulty memories. We only think about the good when we use our experience as a factor in decision-making. We should go back and think as deeply as we can about the negatives as well. You might have fond memories of a car of a certain brand because you learned to drive in it, when in reality it broke down every other week.

The memories, not the experiences themselves, call the shots. That in itself tells you how off-base our decisions can be. Even if you've gone through something, you have to make sure to consider, at the least, the average of the experience, not just the peaks and crests that represent the best of times. It wouldn't hurt to also remember the valleys and nadirs that represent the worst of times as a cautionary tale.

Overall, decision traps and cognitive biases reveal one truth about human beings. We want to operate as if we are correct and understand the truth. This is highly positive and optimistic thinking, but it can also be called hubris and arrogance at the same time.

How can you fight these biases from entering into your decision-making? It's a matter of stepping back and first looking through these chapters to make sure you aren't committing grave sins. Honesty is key in this step. Then you must begin to ask yourself the following foundational questions that underlie your beliefs and reasoning:

1. Can you articulate your reasoning coherently without emotion or "hunches"?
2. How valid are the cons and arguments against your belief and reasoning?
3. *What* do you think influences your beliefs?

4. If all factors were equal, is this still the belief you would hold, or are you influenced by something external?
5. What do you gain and lose with this decision?

Cognitive biases and decision traps don't represent a deviation from normal thinking— they *are* normal thinking. Keep that in mind the next time you think you are being clear-minded.

Takeaways:

- Cognitive biases are actually the most natural and instinctual way of thinking, which is bad news for your decision-making muscle. This chapter represents four more common cognitive biases that will cause suboptimal decisions.
- Unconscious bias is being ruled by the stereotypes we hold about people, places, and things. They are basically assumptions, but we don't know that, and we act on the stereotypes instead of looking at the situation at hand.

148

- Confirmation bias is when you see or interpret things only to bolster your pre-existing assumptions and beliefs. This can cause, in a word, blindness.
- The gambler's fallacy is when you try to find patterns in random, chaotic events that you have no control over. There is a lack of using actual evidence.
- Rosy retrospection is when you emphasize the positive nature of a past experience and apply that incorrect assessment to a current situation. Your biased memory calls the shots here, not your wealth of past experiences.

Chapter 8. How to Beat Analysis Paralysis and Indecision

For some of you, this might be the only important chapter of the book. How can you deal with indecision—the bane of so many people's lives?

Analysis paralysis isn't just a fancy, rhyming term. It's a real problem that can keep you from everything you hold dear in life, personal and professional. It's when, despite having all the information at your disposal, you are paralyzed. Perhaps it's *because* you have such a plethora of information, or perhaps it's because you don't actually know what is best for you. Regardless, you can't make a choice and you stall until you suffer the consequences for not taking action or until someone else throws their hands up in disgust and makes the decision for you.

Why do we have such an aversion to making decisions sometimes? Are we really frozen simply because of the paradox of choice? Interestingly enough, people who feel that they are indecisive aren't so in all aspects of life. It is usually confined to a certain area that they don't feel confident in.

This is one of the major reasons for indecision. When we make a decision, we are owning it and putting ourselves—our intelligence, creativity, fitness, musical talents, you name it—on the line for evaluation and judgment. For every positive reaction to a decision, there is a negative one, whether real or imagined. We absolutely hate the idea of being looked at in a negative manner, even if we're completely right. Making a decision opens you up to that can of worms, at least when you're making decisions for or in front of a group.

In other words, it doesn't usually come down to decision fatigue or trying to optimize for the best option, although it can certainly be an issue from time to time. The biggest reason most of us are indecisive is because we don't want people to think we're stupid. It's often a confidence issue as opposed to a pickiness issue.

For instance, let's take the all-too-common scenario of having to decide what restaurant to eat at with a friend. You might feel hesitant to choose a place because you feel like you're in a no-win situation. You want to please and accommodate them and make sure your choice of restaurant isn't judged. If you choose a place not to their liking, you imagine they will think you are both (1) stupid and (2) inconsiderate to their taste.

This in a nutshell illustrates the most common feeling of analysis paralysis. It sounds far-fetched, but when we make decisions outside of a vacuum and in the real world, your decisions say something about you to other people. If you feel like you can't win, you stay still in the hopes that you'll do less damage that way. At the very least, it can feel like an exhausting chore. That's where the instinct to dig your head into the sand like an ostrich can come from.

This notion is parallel to what we call "planning paralysis"—when planning becomes a higher priority than actually *doing* something. The job of *planning* to leave your comfort zone takes precedence over, or at least valuable time from, your actual project.

Planning and analyzing are comfort zones, not just because you can do it from a couch. To do something, you have to get outside and risk a certain vulnerability. So it's always easier to keep planning, because technically it's useful to your task. You can lead yourself to believe you're being productive toward making a decision.

Planning to map out precision and sewing up random details isn't the worst way to go about projects. But more likely, planning is a device that helps one avoid action to mollify our fears and anxieties. When we're spinning our wheels, it's because we've started listening to that inner voice that likes to harangue us into believing all we do will fail and we're foolish for trying.

Listen up, indecisive people and those of you who are struck with analysis paralysis. What follows are some tips for you to pull the trigger more quickly and confidently. You may have imagined you had to sacrifice one and you couldn't have both, but it's not true.

Taking Action

First, realize that almost every decision is reversible and you can take them back to some degree. Therefore, it makes sense to dip your toe into one option to see what happens and gain some information instead of standing at the fork in the road until you starve to death. You learn so much more by acting as if you are going to take option B instead of hemming and hawing about both. It's only in the process of option B will you learn more about it and how it feels.

If you are trying to decide between moving to New York or Texas, are you going to gain more information by visiting neither and continuing to debate with yourself or by visiting one, seeing how you feel about it, and going through some motions to gain information? The point is that taking a few steps down one road is extremely reversible and worthwhile due to what you'll learn.

Second, as we discussed in an earlier chapter, apply strict boundaries to help you make the choice for you. It streamlines your process and reduces the amount of thinking you have to do. For example, if you are struggling with what restaurant to pick for dinner, you might apply filters of healthy, inexpensive, within a 10-minute drive, and not hamburgers. After you set these boundaries, you might only have one or two choices left over. It's like when you shop online and apply filters for size, style, price, and color; suddenly you're left with only two shirts to buy.

If you're left with zero choices, remove one or two filters and work backward until you can make an easy yet satisfactory choice. You'll be left with choices that are within your criteria, and at that point, what does it matter? You can choose at random at this point with no loss in happiness or effectiveness, and you've successfully ignored everything that you *don't* care about.

A corollary to setting boundaries is to first decide upon a *default choice* if you can't decide within a set amount of time. Pick your default upfront, then set a time limit, where if you can't choose something else, you automatically go with the default. For instance, with your significant other, your default restaurant is an Italian joint. If you can't choose a different restaurant within five minutes each night, then to Italy you go. This saves time, but the act of creating the default choice is important because you will have automatically selected something that fits your requirements or desires. You'll be happy in either case, in other words.

In many instances, the default is what you had in mind the entire time and where you were probably going to end up regardless of going through the motions and endless debate. You go through the mental exercise of choosing a "default" with the idea that you might end up there anyway.

Third, realize that you might have a drive to make the "perfect" decision. This is similar to what we've talked about previously with satisficing versus maximizing decisions, but it differs because perfection is about something that doesn't exist.

If something checks all your boxes, that's all you need to beat your indecision. When you aim for perfection, you also tend to start running up against the law of diminishing returns, which states that the amount of effort you put into something isn't worth the return you gain anymore. For example, you might spend a $100 on a pair of nice shoes. At that price point, they will be well constructed, sturdy, and fashionable. What if you were to spend $200 on a similar pair of shoes? They'd still be well constructed, sturdy, and fashionable.

This begs the question, were they worth the extra $100 over the cheaper pair? For most people, no. There is a law of diminishing returns where the more expensive shoes don't make a difference in any relevant way. How nice can a pair of shoes get? Unless the more expensive shoes are self-cleaning with automatic lacing, you are spending more for essentially the same return.

You probably aren't shooting for life-changing restaurants every night of the week. In this case, your compulsion to make a perfect choice is wasted energy. Eating is the goal, not choosing a perfect meal. Unless you are making life-impacting choices that you will feel the repercussions of for years, attempting to make a perfect choice is silly. The difference between the "perfect" choice and the "good enough" choice will be negligible, and you might not even feel it, or remember it, the next day. There won't be consequences that make a difference in the long-term, so what is the sense in spending additional time on it?

A famous comedian has clever input on this matter: "My rule is that if you have someone or something that gets seventy percent approval, you just do it, 'cause here's what happens. The fact that other options go away immediately brings your choice to eighty, because the pain of deciding is over." This is surprisingly similar to what former U.S. Secretary of State Colin Powell has to say on the matter, as discussed later in this chapter.

Fourth, to make better and quicker decisions, engage in intentionally judgmental thinking. This is the type of thinking you have probably tried to repress, but it will be very beneficial for your decision-making. Think in black and white terms and reduce your decisions down to one to three main points.

Overgeneralize and don't look at the subtleties of your options. Willfully ignore the gray area and don't rationalize or justify statements by saying "But..." or "That's not *always* true..."

The idea is to focus on what really moves the needle for you and ignore things that, while they matter, aren't the most important things. Sometimes, consuming less information will help this because you are focused on a smaller set of factors.

Let's go back to the example of choosing a restaurant for dinner. How can you think more in black and white terms about something like this?

Simply reduce your restaurant choices down to what you might categorize as a first impression. Restaurant A is a place for burgers, despite the fact that there are five menu items that are not burgers. It doesn't matter—in black and white terms, it's a burger place.

Restaurant B is expensive, despite the fact that it has five items that are cheap. It doesn't matter—in black and white terms, it's expensive. Restaurant C is far away, despite the fact that if you hit good traffic, it's not too far. It doesn't matter—in black and white terms, it is far.

Seeing options in black and white terms basically generalizes their traits and removes their subtleties. Remember, if we're talking about destroying indecision, this is one of the best things you can do. If you have a hazy stereotype of your two options and the stakes are relatively low, then that's all the information you need.

A final method to be intentionally judgmental is to sum up your options in one short sentence only, no commas or addendums allowed. You aren't allowed to elaborate on anything. When you try this, you'll notice you can only end up with broad strokes, such as "It's a burger place that's 10 minutes away" versus "Well, they serve burgers, but they also have lasagna and tacos. It's 10 minutes away, but I think we can get there faster." Which one is going to be easier for you to ignore or accept?

The 40–70 Rule

As promised, another corollary that relates to Louis C.K.'s statement that 70% is the golden number to hit.

Former U.S. Secretary of State Colin Powell has a rule of thumb about making decisions and coming to a point of action. He says that anytime you face a hard choice, you should have *no less* than 40% and *no more* than 70% of the information you need to make that decision. In that range, you have enough information to make an informed choice but not so much intelligence that you lose your resolve and simply stay abreast of the situation.

If you have less than 40% of the information you need, you're essentially shooting from the hip. You don't know quite enough to move forward and will probably make a lot of mistakes. Conversely, if you chase down more data until you get more than 70% of what you need (and it's unlikely that you'll truly need anything above this level), you could get overwhelmed and uncertain. The opportunity may have passed you by and someone else may have beaten you by starting already. The law of diminishing returns starts to hit hard at this point.

But in that sweet spot between 40% and 70%, you have enough to go on and let your intuition guide your decisions. In the context of Colin Powell, this is where effective leaders are made: the ones who have instincts that point in the right direction are who will lead their organization to success.

For our purposes of making decisions, we can replace the word "information" with other factors: 40–70% of experience, 40–70% reading or learning, 40–70% confidence, or 40–70% of planning. While we're completing the task, we'll also be doing analyzing and planning on the fly, so this range of certainty helps us tend toward action.

When you try to achieve more than 70% information (or confidence, experience, etc.), your lack of speed can result in many negative consequences. It can also destroy your momentum or stem your interest, effectively meaning nothing's going to happen. There is a high likelihood of gaining nothing further from surpassing this threshold.

This way of thinking leads to more action than not. Making the decision before you're 100%—or even halfway—ready to do so is the kind of move that kicks you into action.

Beating analysis paralysis in general is a matter of understanding why you feel mired among choices and taking perspective into account when you think about how much time you are spending deciding versus how much additional joy you'll receive. Setting boundaries to find essentially equal choices helps, as does seeing only in black and white.

Takeaways:

- Indecision is a tough beast to beat, but it's not always a matter of having the right tactics or avoiding the paradox of choice. Much of the time, we are indecisive because we are afraid of what our decisions will say about us to others. We are afraid of the judgment, plain and simple. Thus, we fall into analysis paralysis or planning paralysis.

165

- One method to beat indecision is to walk down one path, but to the extent that it is reversible. It gives you more information than you would have otherwise and forces action, which is the name of the game.

- You can also set boundaries or filters based on one or a few restrictions to help you get to a decision point more quickly. This can quickly turn your cornucopia of choices into a select few. Another application of filters is to choose a standing default choice, which you will use if you can't decide within a given amount of time.

- Being judgmental is bad, but being intentionally judgmental and painting with a broad stroke can make decisions much easier. This works by removing the subtleties and making you focus on one or two factors.

- The 40–70 rule is a final way of forcing action and a decision. It states that you should make a decision when you have no more than 70% of the information or gumption that you feel you need. Chances are that you are suffering from the law of diminishing returns at that point, and you know more than you need already.

Chapter 9. Inevitable Emotions

Human beings aren't machines, even though sometimes life would be easier if we were.

It's been implied more than a few times that the presence of emotion can be highly detrimental to your decision-making. You probably don't have to look any further than the last time you were in a poor mood to see what you ate in an attempt to make yourself feel better. Why is there usually a push to eliminate emotion from the thought process?

First, emotion tends to make us disregard logic, and many see cold logic as the ultimate tool for making decisions. We figure logic will never lie to us the way an emotion might. In fact, the stronger the emotion, the more we are blinded to what's in front of us. Logically, you might understand that you need to eat better, but if you feel anxious and tired from a long day at work, you might splurge on a dozen donuts.

Second, emotions don't always relate to the reality at hand. You might feel a certain way about something and project those feelings onto your current situation. If you feel angry about your spouse, you might in turn make a decision at work that indicates bitterness to someone else. Put simply, events cause our emotions, and our emotions cause events. They aren't always conscious, and we don't always match them up correctly. There is considerable room for misinterpretation.

Finally, different emotional states can cause us to look at the same situation from 10 different perspectives. Suppose you don't like dogs. You find them bothersome and annoying. Then suppose you watch a commercial with sad-looking kittens and puppies, and a narrator says there is a possibility they will be euthanized. Will your view change at all, however slight?

Appropriately, emotion is usually characterized as an obstacle between you and optimal decisions, but interestingly enough, research has found that you literally can't make decisions if you are emotionally impaired. In other words, you need emotions to guide your decisions much like you need taste buds to guide your sense of taste.

Can't Live with Them, Can't Live Without Them

Studies in the early 1990s by Portuguese neuroscientist Antonio Damasio proved what happens when you remove all emotion from the decision-making process. Specifically, he observed what happened when one of his patients, Elliot, had parts of the ventromedial frontal lobe of his brain removed because of a tumor.

Coincidentally, this is the part of the brain that handles emotional processing. Before the surgery, Elliot was married and successful in his career. He also boasted a 97th-percentile score for his IQ. He was by all measures an intelligent man that was primed for long-term success and happiness. What happened to Elliot *after* the surgery?

His marriage fell apart. His career began to take a nosedive, and any subsequent businesses he started were unsuccessful. Elliot lacked motivation and drive to do anything, and he seemed content to let his life pass him by as an "uninvolved spectator." Damasio discovered the problem at the root of everything was Elliot's inability to make decisions, trivial or complex.

Even the smallest decisions would take Elliot an inordinate amount of time, such as making an appointment, choosing where to eat lunch, and even deciding what color pen to use. He was normal in all other ways, but his lack of emotions made him completely apathetic about the decisions in his life.

We might believe that we make our decisions rationally or logically, but the truth seems to be that it's mostly an illusion. It's an illusion that might allow us to make better decisions, but emotions are always in the background, coloring our perception without our conscious realization.

If you completely suppress your taste buds, you lose the ability to taste. At that point, what drives your food preference? If you lose your sight, what drives your scenery preference? You can't remove emotion from the decision-making process because it's part of your personal logic.

The same theme keeps popping up: we think we know what we're doing, but it turns out we are just marching to the drum of our subconscious.

There is no better demonstration for the separation of how we wish to act versus how we are subconsciously influenced to decide than Professor Robert Cialdini's famous methods discussed in his seminal book *Influence*.

Cialdini discussed six weapons of influence that underlie many of our decisions and subtly persuade us into a certain direction. They tug on our heartstrings and manipulate our emotions, undercutting our logical assessment of the situation. His influence factors are as follows:

1. Social proof
2. Liking
3. Reciprocation
4. Scarcity
5. Authority
6. Commitment

Social proof is taking a cue from other people to make our decisions. If we observe others leaning a certain way, then we innately will as well because "if so many people are doing it, they can't be wrong," even though they clearly can be wrong. You can also think of this as the mob mentality at work. Monkey see, monkey do.

Liking takes something you've known your whole life and makes it official. We are more easily persuaded and influenced by people we like, people we find attractive, and people who seem to like us. We feel that they have our best interests at heart and that we can trust them more. This is why celebrity spokespeople are so popular and effective.

Reciprocation takes advantage of the fact that when someone is nice to us, we immediately feel an emotional debt and the compulsion to pay them back. When someone does us a favor, it's natural for us to seek ways that we can perform a favor for them. You'd feel bad if you didn't—that's emotional debt.

Scarcity fuels all attractive sales such as "limited time offer" or "prices shoot up at midnight." Scarcity is when you are compelled to a decision because something seems to be low availability, but it really means that you are driven by your need to not miss out on something, rather than a need to do something. Scarcity makes you reactive to a situation rather than proactive.

Authority figures are theoretically in their positions because they know best, so we heed their words. Whenever we see someone that we perceive to be in authority, we disproportionately weigh the importance of their words, often without question, because we assume that they know much better than we do.

Commitment plays on the fact that we all have a certain self-image about ourselves, and we like to act in ways to further that self-image. If we want to be seen a certain way, we will commit to that image with consistency. For example, you would feel compelled to give a donation to charity if you are often asked if you are a kind, charitable person.

These six persuasion methods add fuel to the fire that we are driven by subconscious emotion more than we like to admit. It might end up in suboptimal decisions from time to time, but completely removing emotion is to become a spectator in your own life. A typical emotional decision is extremely fast. Studies have quoted figures around 0.1 seconds. This was necessary to activate your fight-or-flight instinct to simply keep you alive. It's what creates the "hunches" or gut feelings we sometimes have.

However, most of us (and certainly if you're reading this right now) don't live in that kind of world any longer. So what's the use? As author Jonah Lehrer put it, "The human brain (the 'rational' brain) is like a computer operating system rushed to market with only 200,000 years of field testing... it has lots of design flaws and bugs. The emotional brain, however, has been exquisitely refined by evolution over the last several hundred million years. Its software code has been subjected to endless tests, so it can make fast decisions based on very little information."

The logical rational brain is relatively new and still doesn't know what to look for, but the emotional brain has millions of years of information and experience to react to. That might say it all about emotional decision-making. Try as we might to be impartial or coldly calculating, it's impossible to ignore the instincts that kept human beings alive.

You can make the subconscious a little more conscious by actively asking if you are being influenced by any of Cialdini's persuasion factors in your decisions. Do you actually want that new sweater, or do you just not want to miss out on a low price? They are very different desires.

You can also make effort to identify the emotions and assumptions that influence your decisions. Instead of ignoring or repressing your emotions, bring them into the light and see them for what they are. We don't do this often because we fear judgment—even from ourselves. However, burying your emotions robs you of important information to make decisions with. If you don't want to look at your thoughts, you can easily look at your actions to indicate your emotional state.

The real factors that convince decisions are emotional. Logic is far less reliable because it assumes that people will see things your way. Emotions, however, are universal and easier to evoke and manipulate.

Finally, you can attempt to think as if you were an innocent bystander that was thrust into the tough bind you are currently in. This is otherwise known as the act of disassociation. What factors would you look at, and what would you ignore? Are they different from what you're thinking about right now, or is there considerable overlap?

The reason this is an important perspective to channel is that you are likely too emotionally invested and affected. No matter the situation, you bring your own experience into it and possess a personal stake. This type of emotional investment means that you will focus on emotional factors rather than the facts at hand. You will examine every little detail that affects your emotional state, details that don't actually matter in the grand scheme, and details that aren't decision-worthy.

The most common example here is when you listen to a friend ranting and raving about their poor romantic relationships. You'll notice that you will get an abundance of details, and all are supposedly key to the narrative that they are describing, but they aren't. You can probably sum up their entire story in a few sentences without mentioning the tiny details they keep expounding upon.

The reason they are doing so is because they think their situation is different and special, but it probably isn't. They might be agonizing over mixed messages sent via text messages while ignoring the fact that they haven't seen them in weeks.

This type of insight is only possible when you try to disassociate from the situation at hand and think like you would be advising an impartial third party. What would you focus on and what would you ignore? It will become far clearer.

Tame Your Ego

We might not like to admit it, but our ego plays a bigger role our decisions than we like to think.

When we talk about the ego, it generally means we are making decisions out of a place of fear, preventing loss, and maintaining security for ourselves. That might sound like a reasonable approach to have, but if your primary metric in making decisions is to make sure that you are psychologically protected, imagine what you will miss out on because of fear and how dishonest you allow yourself to be.

Put another way, the ego is how your sense of self-esteem acts to protect itself. The ego analyzes reality and provides an explanation for your self-esteem to remain as intact and healthy as possible for better functioning. We may not receive an objective view of reality if our ego has anything to say about it.

If one were to truly view all of their failures in

their life as solely their own responsibility, it would result in someone feeling despondent about their ability to even wake up in the morning. We need our ego to feel good about ourselves and function on a normal level. But how much is too much? When does ego begin to negatively influence our decisions?

It happens when we make decisions solely to protect our psyche with defense mechanisms and keep our self-esteem high. Let's take a look at some of the most prevalent defense mechanisms you may or may not be aware of and see how they can influence your decisions.

Blaming. If you constantly blame others for your negative outcomes, it means you don't have to take responsibility for them. If it wasn't your fault, then you are not deficient whatsoever; you were just a victim in an otherwise negative situation. This is also known as deflecting responsibility to someone else and viewing yourself through an external locus of control: the idea that you can't control your actions and surroundings and that they are the result of external forces acting upon you.

Blaming affects your decisions because it ensures you will never learn from them. If you don't believe that you are at fault, then why would you want to change anything?

Denial. Denial is a powerful defense mechanism. Denial is when you simply refuse the negative conclusion about yourself. You can do this in many ways.

You can simply refuse to believe it and construct a narrative that it is incorrect, far exaggerated from the truth, or based on a technicality. "No, I eat healthy," when in fact you eat McDonald's five times a week.

You can refuse to believe it on the basis that it only applies in certain circumstances. "No, I eat healthy every day. Minus the weekends, for which Friday counts." You can even accept it and refuse it simultaneously by acknowledging the poor outcome yet rationalizing the reasons and excuses why it was unavoidable for anyone, including you. "No, I eat healthy. I just can't resist sometimes when I see candy, but I'm healthy besides candy."

As you can see, the possibilities are endless in constructing a denial argument. The only thing in common is that you are absolved of all wrongdoing and your self-esteem is protected because you don't acknowledge your own behavior.

Denial affects your decision-making because you may have no idea of your true capabilities. It makes you blind to what is actually happening, and you might be blindsided by negative consequences even though the signs were right in front of you the whole time.

Rationalization. This is when you come up with a reason for every failure that wasn't your fault.

This is a problem especially with smart people and those that are good at arguing. They are able to argue with themselves and convince themselves of the logical reason they created. This allows you to deflect things away from your ego with a seemingly plausible explanation.

Wherever a bad decision is made that would reflect poorly on someone, there is a rationalization to be had—a reason that makes it okay in your mind.

If you break a chair, you simply rationalize that you wanted to buy a new set anyway. If you punch someone, you rationalize it was because they deserved it and had it coming. If you fail at talking to the opposite sex, you rationalize that it doesn't matter because they were ugly or boring anyway.

You keep your self-esteem protected, but it puts your decision-making skill into a huge blind spot. You can be making clearly bad decisions, feel the sting of the negative consequences, and still rationalize to yourself that you did the right thing.

You may not understand or connect the dots, which sets you up for continued failure in the future.

We want to look good in front of others so they might like us more, and we sometimes resort to almost anything to achieve that. If this is the main issue on your brain, you operate based on the emotion of fear and anxiety, and any critical thinking will go straight out the window.

Decisions are best made when you know what influences you are operating under. The ego is so instinctual and natural for some of us that it's hard to separate whether we are acting to protect it or out of our actual free will and opinions.

It's only when we can take the ego into control and realize that being wrong is a completely natural and humanizing trait that we can improve our decision-making.

Zero-Based Thinking

You'd have to be a robot to be capable of making decisions that are completely devoid of feeling. You can, however, learn to identify when your emotions are negatively impacting your ability to make rational decisions and remove them from the equation.

Professional poker players—at least the successful ones—are a good example of this. To win consistently at poker you have to be able to calculate the odds and use that information to decide when to play and when to fold, but even the best poker players are vulnerable immediately after winning or losing a big hand. A big win can make you feel invincible, whereas a large defeat can entice you into chasing your losses.

It's called being "on tilt," and its effect is so hard to resist that some players will deliberately fold the hands following a significant game rather than run the risk of making an unwise, emotion-fueled decision.

Zero-based thinking is a decision-making process based on imagining yourself back at the point before particular decisions were made and is being free to make those decisions with the knowledge that you have now about their outcome. In other words, "Knowing what you know now, would you make the same decision again?"

Knowing everything you know now, would you do the same thing or do something different? Would you go down the same path as you did before? Would you engage in this activity again? Ask yourself these questions to every key area of your business and life. The significance of this is that it allows you to ignore the emotions involved and forces you to answer an easy question.

If the answer to this question is no, then the very next step is to ask yourself "How do I get out of this and how fast"? In other words, revert to zero and start from scratch. Answering no to this question is an indicator this activity or relationship or situation no longer suits you or is in your best interest.

- "If she wasn't your girlfriend, would you get into a relationship with her again?"

- "Would I buy this again if I didn't own it right now?"
- "You pursued the app and gave it your all. If we could go back in time, would you start the app again?"

Have you heard the expression that hindsight is 20/20? We say this when we want to express regret over a bad decision. Well, it's exactly because hindsight is so valuable that we should take note of it. We can't use it to change the past, but we can use it to make smart decisions, right now, for our future.

It's natural to place value on our decisions and sunk costs. Getting rid of something into which we've put time and effort can be difficult to do, even if rationally we know that investing more time and money is only going to mean more waste. Zero-based thinking helps us eliminate our emotional attachments and make the right choices for our business and for our bottom line.

Takeaways:

- Emotions are an inevitable part of the decision-making process. You might suppose that they should be completely shut out, but this would be a mistake as proven by Damasio's studies on Elliott. Therefore, the idea is to control your emotions and try to regulate them.

- You can regulate your emotions by making the subconscious a bit more conscious, disassociating yourself, and thinking as an innocent bystander.

- Another key component of your emotions is taming your ego, because defense mechanisms such as blaming, denial, or rationalization all give you significant blind spots for decision-making.

- Zero-based thinking is where you answer the simple question of, "If you knew what you knew today, would you make the same decision again?"

Conclusion

It's now clear to me how the apartment situation I suffered from in the introduction of this book could have easily been avoided. I had imperfect information and was under a large load of stress. You know by now that those are factors for failure, no matter how well intentioned I was.

Good decisions may seem like something you can master if you just pay attention to what you're doing and think about the consequences. Unfortunately, that's not true.

The real key is to think about what you're thinking and pay attention to what you're paying attention to. That was a tough sentence to read, and it's a tough concept to excel at.

It might seem like the most optimal method is to carry around a giant checklist whenever you are making a decision of note and be completely apathetic on trivial decisions. The latter part is truer than the former, but these will all become instinctual over time.

We started the book with a story about imperfect information, and it's time to realize that you will almost never have perfect information to make decisions with. That doesn't mean you can't keep trying.

Best of luck,

Peter

Summary Guide

Chapter 1. What Drives You?

- Often, decisions can be consciously articulated. If you want Chinese food for dinner, that's easy to justify. But for both quicker and bigger decisions, you are likely more influenced by your subconscious than you realize. The importance of knowing potential subconscious influencing factors is thus extremely high to deciphering your actions.
- There are three models of subconscious needs and desires, the first of which is Maslow's hierarchy of needs. He articulates the following needs: physiological fulfillment, safety, love and belonging, self-esteem, and self-

actualization. Identifying your location in the hierarchy is identifying your subconscious needs.

- The next model is Tony Robbins's six needs: love and connection, certainty, uncertainty and variety, significance, contribution, and growth. Unlike Maslow's hierarchy, these needs function like traits and are present in different quantities in people. Pinpoint your particular needs and understand your decision process better.

- The final model is the Max-Neef fundamental needs: subsistence, protection, affection, understanding, participation, leisure, creation, identity, and freedom. This functions similar to Tony Robbins's needs in that these needs are present in everyone but in different quantities.

Chapter 2. Primed for Good Decisions

- The concept of ego depletion is important because it leads directly to decision fatigue. When you reach decision fatigue, your decisions become incredibly suboptimal because you will either become paralyzed or make a rash, unresearched decision.

- How can you preemptively deal with the effects of ego depletion and willpower fatigue? You can time your decisions wisely such that they made only when rested, you can categorize the trivial daily decisions you have and make sure to only allot a trivial amount of time to them, you can treat yourself like an athlete and make sure you are mentally tapering off in preparation of big decisions, you can give yourself more time than is necessary to reduce the role of stress and anxiety, and you can also work on manipulating your transaction costs to make good decisions more of a default option.

Chapter 3. The Six Hats Method and WRAP

- Most of us engage in very little with regards to our decisions. A pros and cons list, perhaps. But this still leaves us victims of your blind spots.
- The six hats method of decision-making implores you to view a fork in the road from six distinct different perspectives. Typically these are represented by colors, but avatars are more illustrative. The six different perspectives to consider are Sherlock Holmes (gather information), Sigmund Freud (emotions), Eeyore the donkey (pessimist), a cheerleader (optimist), Pablo Picasso (creativity), and Henry Ford (information synthesis).
- The WRAP method was devised to specifically address blind spots. WRAP stands for widen your options, reality-test, attain distance, and prepare to be wrong. As you can see, these are not typical ways to approach a decision, though they can serve you well because they represent what is likelier to happen in the real world.

Chapter 4. Making Calculations

- A simple pros and cons list is a big step for many, but it is not the most effective tool without modification. A highly suggested modification is to quantify your pros and cons list, which is where you assign numeric values to each item to get a clear sense of what matters and what your priorities are. After compiling your two lists, you can choose to evaluate the sums in different manners, such as straight addition, or requiring a certain differential to take action.
- The Force Field Analysis method of decision-making is different than other methods because it is purely about whether or not you should make a change or stick with the status quo. It actually measures how successful your change should be by comparing driving and resisting factors. If you are dead set on leaving the status quo, then you can manipulate the factors by boosting the driving factors or decreasing the resisting factors.

Chapter 5. Mental Checklist

- We are always battling our laziness in all aspects of life. With decisions, implementing a simple checklist of sorts can help.

- First, travel into the future with the 10/10/10 rule. This implores you to consider three different timelines in the future and how you'll feel about your decisions at those three points. Ideally, you want all three timelines to be positive; if not, can you live with the informed decision that one timeline might be negative or detrimental?

- Another mental check-in is to examine whether or not your options are in line with your worldview, and this is accomplished by asking a series of questions that both alleviate you of your blind spots and make clear the reasons you have for engaging in certain actions.

- Setting your own arbitrary boundaries can help with decisions because they narrow your options. You can set limits and use deal breakers or requirements—they all work to clarify your intentions and work more quickly.

- Are you satisficing or unknowingly trying to maximize every decision you make?

Ninety-nine percent of daily decisions don't require maximization and suffer greatly from the law of diminishing returns. Satisficing, a combination of satisfaction and sufficing, is the key.

Chapter 6. Decision Traps

- Through no fault of our own, there are many ways our brains can actively fool us into suboptimal decisions.
- The first cognitive bias is a preference for simplicity and a distrust for complexity. Sadly, life isn't always so simple. This can lead us to prefer the simpler, more direct option over options that are perceived to be more complex and have hidden factors.
- The second cognitive bias is a reliance on contrast and relative value. This makes us susceptible to terrible decisions because relative value is meaningless to us—the only thing that should matter is objective and absolute value.
- The third cognitive bias is a tendency to avoid losses. The psychological harm of a loss is exponentially that of the

psychological benefit of a gain—thus, we seek to avoid losses in decisions whenever possible, even when it is illogical.

- The fourth cognitive bias is a tendency to reduce risk. This is similar to the tendency to avoid losses. We act to reduce risk because it feels psychologically more comfortable and less stressful, despite usually being a poorer decision overall.

Chapter 7. Decision Traps Part Two

- Cognitive biases are actually the most natural and instinctual way of thinking, which is bad news for your decision-making muscle. This chapter represents four more common cognitive biases that will cause suboptimal decisions.
- Unconscious bias is being ruled by the stereotypes we hold about people, places, and things. They are basically assumptions, but we don't know that, and we act on the stereotypes instead of looking at the situation at hand.
- Confirmation bias is when you see or interpret things only to bolster your pre-

existing assumptions and beliefs. This can cause, in a word, blindness.

- The gambler's fallacy is when you try to find patterns in random, chaotic events that you have no control over. There is a lack of using actual evidence.

- Rosy retrospection is when you emphasize the positive nature of a past experience and apply that incorrect assessment to a current situation. Your biased memory calls the shots here, not your wealth of past experiences.

Chapter 8. How to Beat Analysis Paralysis and Indecision

- Indecision is a tough beast to beat, but it's not always a matter of having the right tactics or avoiding the paradox of choice. Much of the time, we are indecisive because we are afraid of what our decisions will say about us to others. We are afraid of the judgment, plain and simple. Thus, we fall into analysis paralysis or planning paralysis.

- One method to beat indecision is to walk down one path, but to the extent that it is reversible. It gives you more information than you would have otherwise and forces action, which is the name of the game.

- You can also set boundaries or filters based on one or a few restrictions to help you get to a decision point more quickly. This can quickly turn your cornucopia of choices into a select few. Another application of filters is to choose a standing default choice, which you will use if you can't decide within a given amount of time.

- Being judgmental is bad, but being intentionally judgmental and painting with a broad stroke can make decisions much easier. This works by removing the subtleties and making you focus on one or two factors.

- The 40–70 rule is a final way of forcing action and a decision. It states that you should make a decision when you have no more than 70% of the information or gumption that you feel you need. Chances are that you are suffering from the law of diminishing returns at that point, and you know more than you need already.

Chapter 9. Inevitable Emotions

- Emotions are an inevitable part of the decision-making process. You might suppose that they should be completely shut out, but this would be a mistake as proven by Damasio's studies on Elliott. Therefore, the idea is to control your emotions and try to regulate them.
- You can regulate your emotions by making the subconscious a bit more conscious, disassociating yourself, and thinking as an innocent bystander.
- Another key component of your emotions is taming your ego, because defense mechanisms such as blaming, denial, or rationalization all give you significant blind spots for decision-making.
- Zero-based thinking is where you answer the simple question of, "If you knew what you knew today, would you make the same decision again?"

74385923R00115

Made in the USA
Middletown, DE
24 May 2018